Post-World War II Germany was Mary Hanford's world as a young American girl. She was the "fly on the wall" witness to events designed to take down the Krupp Empire, which had been major money behind Hitler. Her lawyer father was part of the team that took over the Krupp mansion – Villa Hugel – where behind-the-scenes efforts were coordinated to, frankly, extract justice on Krupp. Mary had virtual free run of the massive mansion known as Villa Hugel, including access to the one-of-a-kind swimming pool beneath the floors where secret strategies were formulated. The German and American publics never were told what really took place during that effort, which ultimately was a disaster of historic proportions due to a senior American official who had personally known Krupp and Hitler, and not in an unfriendly way.

Swimming at Villa Hugel

Memoirs of an American Girl in Post-World War II Germany

Mary Hanford

Published by UCS PRESS

UCS PRESS is an imprint of MarJim Books
P.O. Box 12797
Prescott, AZ 86304-2797

Cover design by Marti Dobkins

Printed in the United States of America

ISBN: 978-0-943247-78-6

Dedication

To the father of Hannah, without whose help, this book would not have been written.

Swimming at Villa Hugel

Memoirs of an American Girl in Post-World War II Germany

Mary Hanford

About the Author

Mary Hanford was born in Washington D.C., a city noted for its international connections, and which symbolized a life marked by travel in Europe, Asia and Africa.

Just before she turned ten years old, her father obtained an important diplomatic position in post-war Germany as head of the British/American Coal Commission, the allies' attempt to bring heat to devastated Northwest Germany.

The Coal Commission's offices were in Villa Hugel, the industrialist Krupp's mansion. Because her parents were absorbed by diplomatic duties, Mary Hanford made close German friends and took them with her to the swimming pool in Villa Hugel and also formed bonds with the servants who looked after her.

Those three years imprinted in her an international outlook and an awareness of moral ambiguities despite nationalities. Later, she became a college professor and author and traveled teaching on Fulbright grants, Global Perspective grants and directed several student abroad programs. She has published over fifty poems, a poetry collection, *Holding to the Light*; also, a critically-acclaimed first novel, *Dr. Sally's Voodoo Man*.

Table of Contents

Chapter One

Georgia To Germany

I. From Georgia to Germany

At the second bus stop, tiny daisies poked their heads up in a vacant lot, so I picked them. "We go to Germany, we do not. We go to Germany, we do not," I chanted and then tossed the daisy petals out the bus window. If Daddy got that job, then Mommy wouldn't worry and Daddy would eat. I knew this because Mommy's face lines smoothed out when she mentioned the "job in Germany." I wanted that job so much that I tried to make it happen by pulling the tiny daisy petals, "We go to Germany, we do not."

To get to school, I had to walk five blocks, take one bus and then give a pink paper, a "transfer" to another bus to get to school. I was in "almost fourth" grade because the Atlanta teacher said I went to a bad school in Washington and didn't learn anything. Daddy was still without a job in Atlanta, so I don't know why we moved, but the pink and white dogwood trees and grass made me happy.

The school was far away because we lived in Decatur on Ponce de Leon Boulevard. "Boulevard," meant a street with a big grassy strip in the center. Across the boulevard lived kids so rich they even had a television. I would gallop over the grassy center to their house, pretending I was riding Black Beauty, so to feel closer to them, for they rode horses.

Decatur was better than Washington where we had lived in a tiny, dirty apartment. Here we shared a big house with another family, Mamie and Albert, who had grown kids, Pat and Bill. Like Daddy, Mamie fell asleep on the kitchen table almost every night, but at least it was after dinner, not before like Daddy. Sometimes, he stumbled upstairs to bed even before me.

Mommy was always cooking, hoping that Daddy might not go to sleep after "refreshments" and would eat his dinner and praise it. "Your father is particular—so brilliant and sensitive," she'd chorus. "No wonder colleagues get jealous—a law degree from Harvard in his teens! A good meal may relax him, help his job search." Then she would stir something. "It's the least I can do," she'd finish. But it didn't happen.

When Daddy got the job, Mommy laughed and held me.

Daddy's new job involved the war. Back then, I had heard of "Hitler," Nazis, and "Japs," on the radio and in movie news reels, but basically war meant sirens and someone yelling "Blackout!" and Mommy's lowering dark shades. War meant something called "rations," which made Mommy wear rayon instead of nylon stockings and buy white margarine lumps with a yellow spot in them instead of butter. I liked to massage the yellow spot until the lump all turned butter color.

But that war had ended so long ago, when I was five. He was supposed to do something with "Krupp," whatever that was.

One afternoon, I came in from playing and heard Mommy and Daddy talking in the sitting room. Usually Mommy was in the kitchen cooking. I went in and sat on Aunt Natalie's needlepoint footstool just to be near the two of them together.

"The British have done a credible job so far in de-nazification. We'd do it differently, of course." Daddy waved his hands; the diamond in the ring on his left hand glinted in the afternoon sun streaming through the window. "Further, it's a good time to be going. Alfried's in jail, and the old man just died in January. It will be easier to get information."

"What old man?" Mommy stirred her drink with her finger, something she'd never let me do.

"Gustav Krupp, of course. I'm surprised you don't know." He raised his eyebrows a little. "Old Gustav was well respected in the area—took care of people. Krupp is a tradition, dynasty really." He held out his empty glass; "We can make inroads with them out of the way. She went to refill it at the chest which held whiskey bottles and ice bucket. "Frances, you really should catch up on what's going on."

I didn't think it very nice to take a trip when someone was dead but didn't say anything because they might tell me to go to bed, especially since I wasn't supposed to sit on Aunt Natalie's footstool. So instead I asked, "Why is the one in jail? Did he shoot someone?"

They both laughed. "In a manner of speaking," Daddy said. "Alfried made bullets, guns for Nazis." Nazis were bad people; that much I knew.

"So that's why he is in jail."

Daddy looked down at me but didn't notice my sitting on the footstool. "Basically, yes, Mary Hanford, but there's more to it…" Then he started talking about other stuff: Russians, Ruhr, on and on, until I fell off the footstool. In a voice that tinkled like wind chimes, Mommy told me to go to bed. When I left, Daddy had drunk only three drinks, and the ice bucket wasn't empty.

Before we left Georgia, my rich friends, Carrie, Sara, and Bob wanted to give me a going away party. I had never heard of a going away party and thought people just went away. The party was out on the lawn on a picnic table. It was covered in pink paper and pitchers of lemonade. Carrie's mother served us white ice cream and even chocolate cupcakes. Afterwards, she gave us little jars with holes poked in the top and we ran around in the twilight trying to catch fireflies. While we chased fireflies, their father came home and both parents sat in lawn chairs smoking cigarettes and having "refreshments." Carrie's father asked me what we were going to do in Germany.

"Well, Daddy's a lawyer, so he'll do lawyering."

"Really?" The father tapped his cigarette into his empty glass.

"Yes. He'll probably make Germans go to court and wear handcuffs." I had visions of monstrous giants turning their pockets inside out and Daddy scooping up cash and coins.

"Is that so?" His laugh sounded deep, like from a well.

"But, really, I don't know."

"He'll probably be in Frankfurt with the High Commission of Germany." He looked out over the lawn as if imagining.

I had no idea what High Commission of Germany meant or that Frankfurt and Essen were cities, but the words sounded so impressive that I said "Sure."

"Well, then..."

"Oh, leave the child alone," Carrie's mother said. "You can find out what you have to in the newspaper."

Just then Carrie burst in on us, her firefly jar blinking in the dusk. "It's 'Howdy-Doody Time,' it's 'Howdy-Doody Time,'" she sang. "Come inside, or you'll miss it. Have you ever seen it?"

"No. We don't have a television." Then we all ran inside.

"When 'Howdy Doody' was over, Carrie's mom passed out favors; mine was a little boat. As I galloped home across the Ponce-de-Leon Boulevard, I reflected on all this celebration for a girl who didn't even live in a whole house. Evidently, since we were going to Germany, we were special. Once we were nobody, now we could be in the newspaper. On Aunt Natalie's footstool, I'd learned that "Krupp" was a family name, that an old man was dead, and that a kid was in jail for shooting someone. I still didn't know what to tell Carrie's dad, but the dogwoods' fragrance and color wrapping the twilight said not to worry.

The next morning, Daddy was sitting in his blue velvet easy chair, reading the *New York Times* and smoking Chesterfield cigarettes.

"Hello, Daddy," I said.

He put down his paper, "Well, Mary Hanford, what is it?" He put his cigarette on the edge of a round bronze ashtray.

"What is your job in Germany? What are you going to do?"

"Hummph." He put his *New York Times* on the end table next to the ashtray but didn't fold it. "You know we had a big war with Germany?"

"Yes, and we won!" I remembered that victory day. Back then, neighbors spilled out of their houses really happy. Some hugged, and some cried. Everyone said Americans were the strongest, best people, so I was very glad to be one.

"Well, 'er yes. Now we have to make sure it doesn't happen again." Daddy leaned back in his chair and crossed his legs. Part of his maroon bathrobe parted, and I could see his striped blue pajamas with a cigarette burn hole in a pant leg.

"Two weeks before your fifth birthday, on June 5th, the Allies divided up Germany and took it over."

"What's Allies?"

"We who fought and won."

"You mean *friends:* people on your side?"

"Yes, so the friends divided up Germany. It is now one part American, one British, one French, and one Russian. Each country is working to rebuild up his German part so it doesn't happen again. There is a rich family named Krupp that has to be dealt with and some other problems. *That's* what I'm going to help with."

So Germany had been divided into slices, like pieces of cake. I wondered if all the divisions were the same, and if they weren't, whether people would fight over it, like kids fight over who has the biggest piece.

"Maybe, Mary Hanford, maybe." He pulled at his chin. "Some of that's already happened, the Russians—some French. Through something called the Marshall Plan, we hope to work together to restore the damage."

"Why would marshmallows help? It would take an awfully lot of them."

His laugh was shrill and surprising, "No, *no!* Marshal, like Mar—shall! It's named after the man who proposed the plan. The Marshall Plan means that the Allies, mainly us, the USA will build back Germany."

"Then why did you tear it down in the first place?"

"We had to. Nazis were very bad people. We had to stop them."

"Then why build it back?"

"So the Germans will become our friends, not stay enemies."

"Yeah, but if you build it back, they can just make trouble again."

"Russians evidently thought the same thing, for they didn't join us. Cordoned themselves off, split the country into two, east and west. We still have a presence in Berlin, but East Berlin is, for all intents and purposes..."

He seemed to have lost the question.

"But why build it back?"

Daddy spoke quickly. "Naturally, we have to make sure bad people who started the war can never do anything like that again. Whatever assets they have left must be confiscated, and that's part of *my* job."

I didn't know what "assets" or "confiscated" meant, but got the main point. "So bad people will be stopped, even though you build it back up?"

He nodded. "Of course, it will depend on how each country wants to handle this."

"I thought the country was Germany."

Daddy chuckled. "I mean the parts that belong to other countries." He stubbed out his cigarette which had toppled into the ashtray. "So, you understand now?"

"Yes," but I didn't. Germany was a country but really two countries because of Russia, but still other countries owned it? If so, then it wasn't Germany any more, whole or split. Or was it like nested boxes; Germany inside a United States box, and Germany inside an England box? It made my head hurt. Probably the situation was more like crepe paper treasure balls, where when as you pulled off the crepe paper layer by layer, you'd find England wrapped in part of it, or Russia or America each time you unwound. Finally, when all the ball was unwound, would be Germany, right at its heart.

But none of that mattered. What mattered was that now Mommy was happy. When I saw her in a red hat trimmed in silver with a tassel hanging down, I knew everything was going to be all right. And it was. When Daddy went to Washington to learn what he was to do in Germany, Mommy put on that red hat and we went "calling." If someone wasn't home, we left little white cards with her name on them. Mostly we went into nice houses and drank tea.

While I sat quiet in a starched dress, Mommy would say "Frank will be using his legal expertise to help the Allies." And then, lifting a little finger over her teacup, she'd add, "It's high time someone discovered him."

II. Lift-Off with Star Fish

The plane had seats like in a movie theatre, just not so many. We sat near the front. Two seats faced us. In them sat two men, one in a trench coat and the other looking really tired. Mommy whispered that the tired man was being "deported." He had done a bad thing so was being kicked out of the United States.

"So what did he do bad?" I asked Mommy.

"Shushhh," she said. "He'll hear you."

Now the media tells of terrorists and boat loads of illegal immigrants being sent back, but then information was not as available. Then I could only imagine what Deport Man had done. He couldn't have stolen war secrets because the war was over. So I guessed he had broken into a house and stolen jewelry or whiskey or looked at a kid sleeping. I had no concept of a "war criminal." Neither was the public much more knowledgeable. "Operation Keephaul," the American and British agreement with the Soviet Union to "repatriate" Germans to the Soviet Union, the **UKUSA** pact to share intelligence, or the rape of Okinawan women by American soldiers were not made public. Such things were shushed, just as I was.

But I had picked up enough about the war and its scrambled aftermath to be worried that everything in Germany would be different, even Christmas. There were bound to be a few Nazis hanging around.

"Can Santa Claus get reindeer into Germany?"

Mommy nodded with her "We'll fix it" smile, and I felt better. After all, our plane had a star on the side, and we were on the way to settle "the damn krauts." Daddy was going to help allies "destroy Krupp," whatever that meant, because how could you destroy a name? Soldiers were laughing about how they "beat the shit" out of Nazis. Americans were Supermen who had rescued people from Nazis, who were synonymous with Germans, and really, really bad. Germans were fierce, like fire-breathing dragons. I didn't know then that Nazis were only a political party that had gotten the upper hand, not a nationality. I couldn't know because most Americans couldn't tell the difference. I did know that Germans were tall, blond and sometimes, square. I had seen them in newsreels, after the man played the organ but before the main feature. Those Nazis probably had things that didn't show in the newsreels, like hawk eyes and claws instead of hands, like the Egyptian god Osiris. More likely, they were like those giant Norsemen who invaded England and tore up gilded manuscripts, the ones I saw pictures of in art class. So how could Santa get into such dangerous territory? Underneath, I also wondered if Santa were real. I'd heard that he wasn't but that parents wanted kids to believe in him, so I played along.

Then the plane began to bump. Bump, whoosh! Rush up, then swoop down. Mommy checked my seat belt. A man said an engine had gone out, but not to worry that we had more left. I didn't worry, but the bumping and whooshing made me vomit, so there was a mess and a smell. On and on went the bumping. Then we swooped really down and landed hard.

The man in the trench coat unlocked the man who was being deported, and they both got off the plane first. As they left, the man who told us about the engine said the plane would get fixed in this place.

"Are we in Germany now?" I asked Mommy.

"No," Daddy said. "We're in the Azores, islands that belong to Portugal."

***

The Azores airport had a small restaurant with only a few chairs and tables, some of them broken. There were no customers, so the waiters just stood around. We went there any way because Daddy said repairs would take longer; the Deport Man had run away, and they had to catch him. The worst part was the bathroom, flies buzzing, poop on the toilet sides and stains on the toilet, on the floor. I wouldn't pee there, but Mommy said there was no place else, so I held it as long as I could. When I finally went, I cried, sure that bugs had crawled into my pants. Even when Mommy looked and said they hadn't, I still cried. So she gave me some money and told me to buy something in the gift shop because then I would feel better.

A gold pin with a navy blue center in the shape of a starfish or a daisy was the only nice thing in the glass-topped counter. I think it was a daisy, not a starfish, because the ends were bent. I bought the pin, but didn't feel any better. Since Mommy thought it might make me feel better, I decided maybe it would make her feel better, so I gave the pin to her.

When we finally got back on the plane, the Deport Man was there, handcuffed again and looking really sad. I felt sorry for him. I slept until another big bump and I heard Daddy say "I'm glad this landing was a bump instead of a splash." Wanting praise for his wit, he looked towards Mommy, and she laughed, but her mouth twitched. I'd not considered that we might crash until he brought it up. When he did, I got goose bumps and wondered if the whole Germany stay might be a bump—or worse, a splash, a drowning. But since we weren't dead or even near dead, I thought about something else.

III. Dieter and Cherries

Later, I stared out the window of the car of the people who met us at the Frankfurt airport. I wanted to look at the so-called monsters. I'd imagined that Germans might be a kind of human/animal, a werewolf type, because they had "goosesteps" and "their claws" in Europe. Daddy said their leaders were "cold-blooded Arians," which sounded like reptilian. The soldiers on the airplane called them "krauts" and "Huns," and either laughed or got mad. I had read about the Huns, especially Attila the Hun, so for sure, Nazis were fierce.

But the Germans on the streets did not look fierce, and I didn't see any claws. Instead, they were pale and spoke a foreign language, not French, the only one I knew. They wore dark clothes and moved with their heads down. Some rode bicycles, but mostly they walked hunched over. It was cold, but some did not wear hats. Maybe they hunched so not to trip on the city's mess. Huge hunks of stone, middle-sized stone, and small bits were scattered or pushed into piles. It looked like giants had slung pottery at each other and then stomped off, crushing church steeples and knocking off roofs. Frankfurt reminded me of the twisted trees in Walt Disney's *Snow White*, the dark, gnarly branches that caught her as she ran and the twisted roots that rose up to grab her.

We pulled up to a building that looked like a big saltine box, only not white with happy red letters, but grey. Outside was a white sign with black letters, "I.G. Farben." Inside people hurried around carrying papers. The offices looked like school principals' offices, except for some were too small—no place for secretaries or assistant principals.

Then we drove way out to a hotel where Germans bowed and smiled like doctors just before giving a shot. A tall, thin pale man whose blond hair stuck out around his ears like a scarecrow shook Daddy's hand. Then a bellhop took us to a room with blue satiny chairs, a big feather bed for Mommy and Daddy and a balcony outside. My bed was in a cutout place under a window. It was warm, and as I lay there, I realized that because Americans were heroes, we'd gotten this wonderful room. I was glad to be American because I could become a hero, maybe like Wonder Woman with a magic lasso and outfit with stars on it. But right then I pretended to be David Copperfield in a ship's hold and that Peggoty had just tucked me in. The ship was rocking on the sea, or Peggoty was rocking me. I heard the slap-slap of waves or maybe—the hum of planes—just before falling off into a dark place.

Light streaming through cracks in the heavy, closed drapes woke me. The drapes weren't closed before so I knew Mommy must be having a migraine. Her headaches always meant a darkened room. As I tiptoed past the big bed towards the balcony, I heard Mommy panting, which made me think of the dog I'd always wanted. When she had a migraine, Mommy usually wanted to be left alone, so I ventured out onto the balcony.

On the balcony red geraniums in pots were looking up at the sun. Below, the same pale, grey people were walking, riding bicycles or talking to each other. What were they saying? Words, like "No, not at all, I would like…" But those words were English, and why could I hear them from so far up?

I couldn't. What I heard was Daddy talking on the sitting room phone.

"I hadn't been in the country five hours before this happened. And there is my daughter…." Then Daddy sounded mad. "Yes, this is urgent! Send one *now*."

Suddenly, I thought I heard Mommy calling and rushed in to help her. It turned out she hadn't, but I stayed by her bed anyway.

Someone knocked on the door and Daddy opened it to the Scarecrow Man who worked downstairs at the desk and an old man wore glasses and smelled of beer, a doctor. He leaned over Mommy with a stethoscope, but I don't know what good it did, because she was still panting. Then he gave her a shot, and she went to sleep. The doctor talked to the tall man who talked to Daddy in English.

"I regret to inform you that Frau Baldy has suffered a heart attack. She must have complete rest, if she is to recover without damage."

"Good Lord, what a time to have this happen!" Daddy slapped his head and then pointed at me. "I have to go to work, you see."

The Scarecrow Man bowed to Daddy and clicked his heels. "I understand, Herr Baldy. We will do our best." But he didn't say what the "best" was. Instead, he and the doctor just left.

Heart attack. Heart attack.

Mommy's brother died of a heart attack. I'd been there when she'd gotten the call about Uncle Pipe, watched as she hunched over the receiver, her head cocked as if bracing herself. "Yes, I know," she had whispered to someone on the line. "I understand."

But I don't think she really understood, but was just trying to be brave. I could tell by the way she took deep breaths and held them. Now cowering in a corner, I took deep breaths.

She'd already had one heart attack, but then I didn't worry. I couldn't tell the difference between that and the migraines which made her vomit and lie in a dark bedroom for days. Dr. McAllister came as usual, but gave her a shot as well as pills. Except for the shot, the only difference between the heart attack and a migraine was that Dr. McAllister came back to the house more times than he did for a migraine. One time he asked to talk to Daddy "apart," so they went into the living room. I listened. He wanted to know if Mommy had been through anything.

Then Daddy told him about Mommy's waking everyone up, yelling that my new friend Jim, a short man with a lined red face, was on the external staircase looking through the window at me sleeping. "Frank, *do* something!" Daddy ran into my room and looked, then went outside, but didn't see him. He told Mommy to calm down, that he would investigate, and he did. He found out the man was on leave from a hospital for the criminally insane. He had beaten up his mother with a tire iron. Because he was crazy, he went to a hospital, not jail. That's what Daddy told Dr. MacAllister.

But then I didn't believe that story. Jim had been visiting his mother, a tiny woman whose eyebrows looked penciled on, but Jim was nice, even if old. He listened to me as I rode up and down. Twice he offered to take me for a ride in his car, but I didn't go. Anyway, why would a hospital let the man visit his mother if he'd hurt her? And was it for sure that he was on the outside staircase? Nobody else saw him. Maybe Mommy just had a nightmare, imagined Jim outside my bedroom window. But Daddy was right when he told Dr. MacAllister that "Frances got very upset," but she probably just imagined that Jim was after me, and so had that first heart attack for nothing.

But in Germany, when I heard "heart attack," I knew the situation was serious. Mommy hadn't had a scare, and treatment could be complicated. Maybe German medicines wouldn't work on her. If they didn't, would she die like Uncle Pipe? Then who would comb my hair, help me write homework, sing to me? A cold feeling ran through me.

"Someone's got to care for her." Daddy pointed at me. "I have to go to work, you see."

"Right," the Scarecrow Man said and then left with the doctor. Before he did, again he clicked his heels. That gave me a funny feeling, probably because of the newsreels.

After a while, he came back with a woman in a maid's uniform. She was young but dumpy with pale brown hair. First, she curtsied; then she just looked at the floor and twirled her hands in her bib apron's pockets. Underneath the bib apron was a faded black dress with short sleeves so tight that her large, muscled upper arms bulged.

Daddy waved at me to go with the woman, but I shook my head.

"You must go, Mary Hanford," Daddy said. "Your mother has to rest. This woman comes highly recommended. She even has a child that you can play with."

"No." I sat down on the floor. I felt like crying, but no tears would come out.

"Don't you understand the seriousness of the situation? Your mother is ill, and I have to work!"

I didn't care if he had to work, but I did care about Mommy.

"It's bad enough when this happens at any time, but in a foreign country, in a war-torn county, it's a disaster." Daddy shook his head.

"What would happen if…" and so on. Daddy kept talking but didn't try to pick me up off the floor. No one did. Finally, the woman took a baby step towards me and held out her hand. The look in her brown eyes was so soft, that I took the hand and let her pull me up. Her palm was rough, like a cat's tongue, but still I didn't let go.

The chambermaid and I walked a long time until we got to a small fenced yard with a shed in the front. Inside the three-walled shed were stacks of logs; outside on one side were more piles of logs, about two or three feet wide. A little further into the yard was a small house, one story with a gable roof. A little boy about five wearing strange leather shorts and suspenders with embroidery on them ran out.

"Dieter." The maid hugged him then we three went inside where a grizzled man with dark hair, wearing the same leather shorts but no embroidery on his suspenders, was waiting. By the way he kissed the woman, I knew he was her husband. Then he scooped up Dieter and they both went out into the yard. The man took an ax and chopped some logs.

They seemed to live mainly in one room, except I had a loft, which judging from Dieter's protests, was really his bedroom. The parents must have had a bedroom somewhere. I was scared and braced myself for battle with the fierce Germans, but the only conflict was over cherries, and I started it.

Supper was on a table pushed against the only window. It was a soup, white with potatoes and looked like a bandage, and dark, fresh cherries. I wouldn't eat the goopy stuff but filled up on cherries. I took out the pits and put them on the edge of the plate which held the soup bowl. Dieter tried the same thing but was quickly told to spit his pit into a spoon, then tilt the spoon on to the plate. Dieter pointed at me with his chubby fingers.

"She's doing it that way, why can't I?" he seemed to be saying.

His parents' tones of voice seemed to say that "*She* may do it that way, but you, Dieter, will be well-mannered. You, Dieter, will spit your seed into a spoon, or we'll know the reason why!"

When I tried to protest for Dieter's sake, his mother responded to my pleas, not by lightening up on Dieter but by showing me to the bathroom.

"No, no," I said when faced with a wooden toilet only to be met with a volley of German. To me German sounded like boots thudding, not terrible but not nice either. I don't remember if I ever went to the toilet that evening, but do recall seeing stars through the small round loft window. I pretended to be a kind of Heidi, who would someday be famous, and so could rescue Dieter if his parents got too mean.

My visit lasted a long time and all during that time, I expected trouble. After all, these were the fierce people and the cherries' quarrel was my fault. But it never happened, not even Dieter sought revenge.

After about a month, Mommy finally got better, so the maid brought me back to my parents. When we left, Dieter stood in the doorway with his thumb in his mouth. His eyes were sad. Later, I really missed Dieter. He didn't tattle, and we played school together.

After a while, I got over Dieter because we were moving. Daddy had to begin his job with the English people in Essen, which is probably why the city started with an E. Daddy's office was to be in a place called Villa Hugel, which had been Krupp's house before he went to jail. Daddy and the English were to "dismantle" Krupp. I thought "dismantle" meant taking apart a fireplace, because Daddy's job also involved coal, a rock that heated places. It might take lots of people to take down Krupp's mantelpiece, which would be huge because Krupp was a big-shot. But "mantle" could also mean "coat," so maybe Krupp had lots of coats.

Despite Dieter and the excitement of moving, the highlight of those first weeks in Germany was that Mommy and I celebrated my tenth birthday on that hotel balcony with geraniums. Mommy took pictures of me, and I took pictures of her. We ate vanilla ice cream from the commissary, and peppermint patties. I didn't have a cake though, or a party and Daddy wasn't there. But I had Mommy; at least I had her.

Back in 1950, all I knew was that one Krupp had gone to jail and that the allies had taken over his house, Villa Hugel, for their offices. I had no idea that the Krupp name meant an ancient armament-making family that provided weapons for both World Wars, and was the lynchpin for armaments for both wars, especially in the early years of World War II. Nor was I told that Krupp industries used approximately100,000 slave laborers, some kidnapped from the east and some from concentration camps, to manufacture U-boats, the "Tiger Tanks" which devastated the allies in Tunisia; and "Dora" the railway from which the Soviet Black Sea fleet was bombarded with 80-centimeter shells in 1941. Naturally, I knew nothing about Krupp's participation in a secret plan to rearm Germany as early as the mid-1930s.

And I wouldn't have understood anyway. When I swam in Villa Hugel's pool and gazed at the large portraits in the Great Room, waiting for Daddy to come from his office, it never occurred to me that I was at the center of power, which like the phoenix, would rise again. The portrait of the Kaiser looked like the one I'd seen in a history book. The tall, white-haired woman in rose wearing pearls, reminded me of my aristocratic grandmother, who demanded I "sit up straight." The men and children were boringly familiar, like Mommy's ancient pictures of relatives, only paintings, not photographs. Nor did I realize that the assets which underwrote the fine house were what Daddy was supposed to make the "Germans turn over." If I had known the scope and difficulty of his mission would I have been more tolerant of his drinking? What he had been given to do would drive anyone to drink, or at least to drink a lot more.

IV. A Haunted House

It was cold, rainy and a long, long car ride to Essen. I read comic books and looked outside at the dark clouds. When we got to Essen, we had to go first to Daddy's office in Villa Hugel, just like we had to go to the I. G. Farben Frankfurt building first. I knew it would be different from the I. G. Farben building because it was way out of the city. First, we went down a long street with tall trees on both sides. Then we drove down a swervy road until we came to another long driveway with lots of flags on tall poles until we got to Villa Hugel, which was a huge mansion. It reminded me of a big, square cake, no—two cakes—because there were two buildings, one big one and one small, connected by a building that served as a walkthrough. If you looked at those buildings sideways, you could imagine it as one double-tiered cake on its side, with the narrow building the column holding up the smaller layer. Whether looking at it straight up or sideways each layer had fancy stuff all around the top like frosting ruffles or rosettes.

But it wasn't a cake and couldn't be, for the buildings were sooty, dark like chimneys of the day. The bare, black trees and grey mansion set against dark clouds reminded me of a haunted house. I got a little scared, but couldn't tell Mommy because a man with two umbrellas came out and took us inside the biggest building.

We stood dripping on the marble floor, while Daddy talked to a man who spoke English in a funny, clipped way. Some lights, like candles, hung from the ceiling in a very, very long room. Despite the lights, there were lots of shadows. As my eyes got used to the dark, I noticed a big space, a hole on the right about midway down the cave; the hole had two columns. Was that hole another building? Was it a dungeon? Just as I thought this, Daddy kissed Mommy on the cheek and told her to go to Ayer House now.

"Does the driver know the way?" Mommy asked. Daddy nodded and started to follow the man with the umbrellas.

I wanted Daddy to say goodbye to me too, not just to Mommy.

"Is your office upstairs?" Daddy nodded again.

"Is there an elevator?" He shook his head and walked into the dark.

As I watched him go, I felt better, even though he didn't kiss me. An upstairs office had to be safer. He wouldn't be swallowed up by the big room with a hole.

V. Fun in the Haunted House

Later, I found that Daddy's office was up on another floor from the Great Hall. I didn't like it up there. The place smelled of cigarettes and had phones ringing, all the time. They weren't real offices anyway because there were no walls, just maps on stands that stood for walls. Between them were desks with papers on them, on the floor and in wastebaskets. The men there almost whispered to each other. There were two women typing, answering phones or filing papers. No one said "Hello" to me, except a secretary named Anna. Instead, most just looked at me like "What is *she* doing here?" I couldn't wait to go downstairs to the pool or just downstairs period.

The Great Hall was beautiful but smelled of bleach and slightly of tobacco smoke, which drifted down from the offices upstairs. Except for the squish of the staff's rubber soles and the clatter of high heels or boots on stairs, Villa Hugel was silent and had a strange sort of chill, one I'd felt before but couldn't remember where.

After I had been in Villa Hugel several times, I realized that the odd chill in the Great Hall was like the one in the mausoleum where I went with Mommy to see Cousin Harriet in a drawer. Mommy scolded me for calling Cousin Harriet's "tomb" a drawer, but that's what it was, one drawer in a white chest of drawers, like the kind they sell in Sears, only bigger. I thought it strange that Cousin Harriet was in this white drawer stacked between many others instead of buried in the ground. How could we know that Cousin Harriet was actually in that drawer, since we weren't allowed to pull it out and look? Mommy said there was no difference between Cousin Harriet resting in this drawer or in the ground because you still couldn't be sure the right person was there. I argued that there was a big difference. In the ground, grass and sometimes flowers, grew above the dead person. Rabbits could run around on top of them and birds could sing. Also being in the ground wouldn't be so *cold*.

"Don't you think graveyards get cold?" Mommy laughed.

"Yes, but not as cold as being up there."

By age six, I'd heard that the dead come back—maybe as zombies or angels, so I worried about Cousin Harriet coming back in that marble box. How would she get out? It wasn't like rising up through graveyard dirt into the air. No, she'd be trapped unless someone heard her making a fuss and came and drilled her out. But it wasn't likely. There were few live people around. The mausoleum was beautiful with carved statues and fountains and lawns. I was impressed by its sunlight, white marble and elegant drawers full of dead people. But even with its sunlight, the place had a strange, unnatural chill.

And in a sense, the dead did come back to Villa Hugel, for I heard talk about those who could have died in battle, who disappeared, who had slaved in the industries. This talk mostly came from Germans, who came to the allies, looking for lost ones, hoping for help. That help involved lots of paper forms and typing. The British and Americans in Daddy's offices talked events not people; the Russian capture of Berlin, the Russian refusal to "unify," the "Berlin Blockade," which I found out meant Allies dropping food over Berlin because Russia wouldn't let people out. Those events which should have been dead were resurrected over and over. No grownup seemed able to let fear go.

Villa Hugel was like that, a beautiful place from which, perhaps, people could never be free. The Great Hall had no white marble or sunlight, but that same chill. However, there were no chests with drawers big enough to hold people, except for two long ones in the basement kitchens. But they held only knives. I know because I looked.

Near the grand entrance stood a wood spiral staircase and under it a suit of armor, which scared me. I didn't dare lift the visor but once touched it with my tongue. It just tasted like a giant soup spoon, nothing special. Behind the stairs was a small oak door and beyond that door lay bare, concrete steps which led down, down to the swimming pool, wonderful, beautiful place which became my castle where I could safely hide. Instead of a moat protecting it, it had iron railings.

VI. The Cleansing Place

Because of the iron railings, you could only get into the pool by wide, long steps in the center, so it was like making a grand entrance. The room was white and green tile, square white tiles on the wall, rimmed every few feet with jade green tile rounds.

Smaller tiles of various greens lined the pool. In an arched alcove perched a white sculpture of a chubby little boy riding an open-mouthed jade fish, his feet on the fish's fins. He was holding a shell in each hand and smiling. I knew he was a boy because of his short curly hair (no one combed it), and his buoyant and aggressive posture. Water gushed out of the fish's mouth, depending on the day's water pressure. The chlorine smell of the swimming pool room wafted through the immense basement kitchens when friends and I rocketed through them to get to the swimming room.

In the pool, I had fun, splashing about, mostly alone, but sometimes with a friend. But no matter how much friends and I battled each other with splashes, the water splashed, never crashed, and then returned to its glassy self. A rotten mango smell suggested mold, but as long as it didn't reach the pool, I didn't care. There was mold in the Kaiser's Shower, where people were supposed to douse themselves before and after swimming. The shower head was rusted, so when we tried to shower, only drops plopped onto the tiny checked white tiled shower floor, plop, clop, slop.

But that didn't matter; because somehow the pool washed away Villa Hugel's unnatural chill. I got warm swimming about, and the cold I felt getting out was just ordinary cold. Villa Hugel's pool became a place where I could hold court with friends, real or imaginary, and where everything seemed normal, like the city pool in Atlanta,

VII. Flowing Outside

Every Friday at Villa Hugel, there was a movie-party in the Film Room, which had a pull-down screen in the middle on which we watched movies. Lots of people and soldiers came on Friday nights. Some people brought drinks from home. There was popcorn, and people to clean up spills. But the popcorn didn't taste the same as in Atlanta. Also, there were candy bars from the commissary. I liked them okay, but preferred German chocolates when I could get them.

Each Friday was a different movie, but still were almost the same. Most had titles with "Flying" in it and airplanes with stars, like the one we came to Germany on. The airplanes were always dropping bombs, and those pilots who dropped them were called "bombardiers." Sometimes, the movies had the same main actor, John somebody. I usually fell asleep before the show was over. Daddy didn't go because he thought the films were stupid.

Daddy and Mommy went to other kinds of parties, grown-up parties. The first party they went to was when we lived in the Ayre House Hotel. It was like Halloween, because they had to wear costumes. Mommy had a long green velvet dress and tall pointy hat with a veil, not like a witch's but like in King Arthur's time. Daddy had knee breeches; white stockings and a vest—blue brocade—like George Washington.

"It's too tight," he grumbled as he buttoned a blue-brocaded vest strained across his pot belly. "Damn nonsense." He reached for a cigarette.

"Now Frank. It's all in fun—and important." Mother brought him a drink; they had set up bottles in their room, almost like they had in Atlanta. Eventually, they left the house with great sweeps, his bowing to her curtsy, just like in the movies.

Later, I heard doors slamming, and pattering on steps. I went to the door of my room and peeped out. Mommy was coming up the stairs, holding up her green velvet gown and crying. No, she was sobbing. Then I heard Daddy stumbling up the stairs as he did in Atlanta.

"God damn bureau-rats! Can't bribe me—don't' care…" and he fell into their bedroom; I heard the thud. This was the first time I'd seen Daddy's drinking affecting anything "outside." Before, any sadness resulted from his not eating supper or at Christmas. Now I knew that the important party was spoiled, at least for them.

After we moved from Ayre house, it became their turn to give parties, which they never did in Atlanta or Washington. Often I sneaked out of bed and sat at the top of the stairs and listened. Like the movies, the parties were almost all the same, but not quite. Usually the British would show up just on time. Eight o'clock meant eight o'clock, and sometimes Mommy wasn't' ready. Daddy would have to fix them drinks until she arrived, usually flustered, from the kitchen. The guests were mostly people Daddy saw every day at Villa Hugel; American, British, and French. The Americans came a little later, and. no matter how much food Mommy had, always brought food or wine or whiskey. French people came even later. The men kissed the ladies' hands; the women would kiss other women two times on each cheek. When Mommy spoke to them in French, they laughed as if really pleased and surprised.

Those who were already friends, loosened ties and leaned against something while talking. Mostly Americans did this. The Brits would nod and say "Old boy." Acquaintances moved from group to group, smiling, patting backs, offering cigarettes, like in a square dance, where you bow and do-si-do, then as you swing your partner you move into another square where you do the same thing.

Despite all the smiles and handshakes, the Americans still seemed the most important, and they chose the British more than the French as friends. The French liked everybody but talked more with each other or Americans than with the British. "The English and the French are old enemies," Mommy told me. "And after all, we saved the French."

At first, the men and women formed separate groups.

"How do you stay so slim?" a woman would ask someone. Other women would ask style advice.

"Etre belle, on faut souffir," one said. Another said style came from the heart. But who would want to suffer just to be beautiful? And if style came from the heart, why did so many women wear the same style? Did they have the same hearts?

The men would discuss Germany, Russia, war reparations, black markets and other boring stuff. Usually they disagreed on how "to handle post-war matters." The British said Hitler admired them and should have known that his blitzkrieg wouldn't work. Hitler might have flubbed the British way, but now German "Anglicization" was taking place. Blind obedience was for dogs, not humans; the British taught Germans fair play as well as that they'd jolly well better not act up again. Americans said when the

Marshall Plan finished rebuilding Germany, these Krauts would know which side their bread was buttered on, would appreciate democracy and free enterprise. The French waved their hands: No, they would not. Look at history. And Germany owed them for devastation centuries back and they wouldn't help one "sou." Instead, Germans must rebuild France!

"Hey, you have a right to what you think, but…" someone would say, but the French would get more excited. Germans *must* pay as a natural consequence of aggression. France would stay loyal, unlike the Soviets, but the situation had to be resolved with justice. Then they would go off on the Russians, like everybody else, how they had refused to "unify," how they had blockaded the Russian sector off, what they would do now….It was like a script, same thing over and over

As for me, I was more worried about getting caught eating the sticks of butter I pillaged from the refrigerator or if Mommy would freak if I talked to an old man with a red, lined face. The only question that bothered me was if Russians invaded, would I ever get a dog?

But, later, at a really fancy party, things got out of hand. At this party, military people wore white uniforms with medals and bars. Mrs. Forquin wore emerald satin, Mommy navy silk ("dark colors hide my fat"). Mme. Pointier was so thin she looked like a pencil in her gold sheath; her upswept brown hair an eraser. Candles glowed all over the house and two extra servants, one to mix drinks, a man who spoke English, and a young woman who passed plates of something before the big meal which was to be at nine o'clock.

At first, everyone was extra polite and talked about HICOG, Krupp, and this time, the terrible "Red Tape." that resulted in "bungling." I had never seen even a sliver of red tape, except on Christmas packages, so wondered at the red tape talk. Maybe Red Tape meant Russians because I've heard them referred to as "Reds." Then I decided it must be a special kind of tape that allies strung along the hidden places in Villa Hugel where I was not allowed. And, in a way, it was.

Later, ugly laughter and loud voices getting louder woke me up.

"We work our goddam guts out to scalp this Kraut, and you tell me they're going to what?" someone yelled.

"Just rumor, Old Boy, can't be true." That voice would be Mr. Merrilees, a British big-shot whose wife was Mommy's friend.

"What? You rescue us from these savages then throw them back at us," Monsieur Garnier said in a muffled giggly tone, like he was smirking. "Russians aren't enough?"

Then Daddy's slurred voice, "Let's look at facts—why would we?" But he didn't finish his sentences. "This isn't possible—just stupid. You do the best you can, then betrayal pounces. Oops, spilled my goddam drink. Get me another drink."

"Even Nuremburg is too soft—gas them the way they gassed…" someone else said.

"You know—after all that, we let the goddam Alfried out!" I recognized Mr. Glass's voice.

Everybody got louder, yelling about Germans, how to "fix them," or "strip them" and what would happen because the American government was too soft as well as wrong, Even Americans started yelling that the government botched something, but I couldn't make out about what, except that it was a particular thing, a mistake.

I put my hands over my ears and dove under the pillow. These three powers were so strong, they could "fix" whatever they wanted. I was scared. *What if someone **really** "fixes them," like they're talking about? Aren't they already fixed? Didn't that happen when we won the war? What's going to happen next?*

But nothing happened next. The morning after, there was usually spilled stuff on the rug and on furniture and lots of crumbs. The place stank of liquor and cigarettes. Glasses with stuff still in them made rings on the tables. Even when the maids cleaned, the smell stayed awhile. Those mornings Daddy didn't go to work and Mommy came down late, looking tired. After a while, I quit listening at the top of the stairs because these parties were boring and also seemed like work—at least for Mommy.

Mommy even had to give parties by herself. Her parties involved cards and winning bridges, even though there were no bridges nearby. This didn't seem practical because if you won a bridge, you'd have to move near the bridge or pay for the bridge to be brought to you, which would be expensive. Anyway, she would set up three or four "card" tables, the only kind of table for bridge parties, and then decorate them. One table would be pink, one green, one yellow—all with flowers. After that she would tell the cook what food to fix, usually cucumber and watercress sandwiches, plus cake. Then Mommy would make "the list." First, she wrote down lots of names, then crossed out some, then added some. She spent a long time planning bridge parties, "for your father's sake." But this didn't make sense either, for Daddy never came to the bridge parties.

When Mommy gave a party, I had to go somewhere else so as not to be in the way. That was okay because when the party was over, all would be cleared away and the air filled with the good smells of dinner cooking. Mommy would be in the living room smoking a cigarette.

"Come here and give me a hug," she'd say, and I would know she was happy with the bridge party. Those were nice days.

But one afternoon I came back early and found Mommy in the living room twisting a lace handkerchief. Her eyes were red and rabbity. I ran to her.

"What's the matter?"

"It's the damn French. There's no pleasing them." She wiped sweat off her forehead as she told me that Madame Pointier was angry, that she blamed Mommy for the seating arrangement and said Mommy was anti-French. As Mommy was telling me how hard she tried and how awful Madame Pointier had been, I was getting mad. I had heard Americans and British complain about the French but *never* Mommy. She had studied at the Sorbonne and attended the Cordon Bleu. She had a master's degree from Columbia in Latin languages and taught French. She loved all things French and often said that it had been a privilege for a country Methodist minister's daughter to study in France. I don't know how she did it, for her family lived in run-down parsonages, and she wore only hand-me downs. When I wanted to irritate her, I would tell her I yearned to marry a minister, just to see her get upset

So why was it so important where Madame had been seated? Parties were supposed to be fun, not contests about who got the best seat. I knew that social position meant a lot to her, and was proud of clubs that bragged about ancestors. It wasn't enough to belong to "Daughters of the Revolution," she topped that by also joining "Daughters of Founders and Patriots," whose members from *both* sides of her family came to America on the Mayflower. Still it didn't seem enough to make her cry so hard.

Mommy was intelligent and educated, but quirk-filled and obsessed with looks, specifically weight. Mommy disdained Jews, divorcees, people who worked with their hands, and people who didn't have anything. She never thought of black people as anything but "help," so I never told of afternoons spent with Jim, our yardman, wishing he were my father.

Now I realize that her cheek's three-inch scar prophesied her life. She had created the three-inch curved scar when she was two and gotten hold of her father's straight-edge blade and tried to shave. Only a forced rescue by a shocked mother kept her from bleeding to death. Over time, that scar became a symbol of self-inflicted wounds resulting from capitulation to male demands on women. First, as a Methodist minister's daughter, she could not dance, drink, smoke or play cards. Second, as a school teacher, she had to be "a role model." Third, as a diplomat's wife, she was responsible for her social status and Daddy's "progress." As the dutiful wife of an alcoholic, she covered for his drunkenness, supported the family, and died young. She followed traditional paths with predictable steps; it hadn't seemed to occur to her to rebel at anything.

But I learned later that Mommy had a secret side. She was able to study at the Sorbonne only because of borrowed money from a beau, Mr. Cassidy, a scandalous risk in her day. Although she held a master's degree from Columbia University, she couldn't get a teaching job, whether because of the depression or because she cared for her sick mother a year after graduation. So to get a competitive edge, she had to go "abroad." Had this loan become public, it would have ruined not only her reputation but that of her stern, protestant father, the Very Reverend Robert Waterfield.

Mr. Cassidy visited once. I was six and he brought me a tiny glass cup and saucer. He wore a grey suit with small stripes and glasses with gold rims. His nails were clean and white, not yellowed, so I knew he didn't smoke. They sat in the living room chatting all afternoon, and I could tell he was still sweet on Mommy. When Mr. Cassidy left, he switched his folded umbrella to his other hand and took Mommy's hand.

"Goodbye, Frances," he said. His voice quivered a little. He never married.

Afterwards, I thought that Mr. Cassidy seemed a splendid boyfriend, and wondered why Mommy had married someone else. Just as I had wished Jim, our yardman, was my father, so I speculated about Mr. Cassidy as a dad. He wouldn't drink anything but lemonade, so he might really play with me.

"Why didn't you marry Mr. Cassidy, Mommy? He seems so nice."

Mommy was bending over the kitchen counter, studying a pickerel and an open cookbook. She looked up and stiffened a little.

"Because he was Catholic." She sighed a little.

"Catholic?" I remembered the crucifix I'd found in her jewelry box when playing dress up. Mommy had said that Mr. Cassidy had given it to her before she went to France, and that it had been "blessed by the pope," whatever that meant. I was upset because it had a man hanging on it. Mommy said Catholics do that and it wasn't important.

But then, that hanging man did seem important. "Were people supposed to suffer?"

"Yes," Mommy nodded, then shrugged. "Daddy's congregation would never have forgiven him."

She began rinsing the pickerel. "Now run along. I only have fifteen minutes before I need to put dinner on." I obeyed but thought her answer a stupid reason for not marrying someone. I still do.

Only when in my twenties did I learn Mr. Cassidy had launched her career by loaning her money and the ramifications of a Methodist minister's daughter marrying a Catholic. And only in my thirties did I learn why she had married Daddy—because she was pregnant with me. My father told me this on his deathbed; she took her secret to the grave. After they were both dead, a cousin told me of Daddy's "confession" to his family of why he had married "beneath him." His confession elicited contempt from the males, who considered his confession "ungentlemanly," but "the females were hard on her." All I knew is that Mommy often left Grandmother's house crying.

But, in Germany, in 1950, when she cried, all I could do was hug her. Maybe that's all I could ever do. After being in Essen a while, I understood that these parties weren't really for fun, but Villa Hugel business flowing outside. Her sorrow was not only, or even chiefly, caused by her need for approval. Mommy's parties were part of Daddy's work, just without maps or papers. Her failure was his failure somehow, and it wasn't fair. Villa Hugel hung over us like a huge grey tent, threatening to collapse and smother us.

Chapter Two

First Winter and Heinz

Ayre House had been confiscated by the allies and was more of a small hotel than a bed and breakfast, for we could take any meal in the dining room. There was a common room with heavy wine-colored drapes, and a long, narrow library. Right off the common room was a dark, leather-clad lounge run by a bartender named Heinz who spoke English and seemed friendly. Everything was brown, except the horseshoe-shaped bar which also had brass nails in it. Upstairs, were lots of bedrooms, but each floor had only one bathroom which was in the hall.

The best part was that I had my own room. It was a big oblong with a single bed with a brown print bedspread against one wall, a "shrunk" against another and lots of light streaming through two tall windows. That light would wake me up, and for a second I would be confused by the clean, airy room. That room was not in the tiny Washington apartment or the half-a-house in Atlanta— then where? Then I would realize I was in Germany with its ruined buildings and green, tall trees, and I would feel happy.

There were only a few regulars, us, two army men, and an American civilian, who had a dog.

We three would eat breakfast in the dining room, usually with Sergeant Nellie, tall and mustached, and Sergeant Dumkowski, short, square and clean-shaven. They wore pressed uniforms and shiny shoes, never complained about the food and always got up when Mommy came into the room, so had to be the heroes everyone talked about. They also joked a lot. Sometimes their jokes took the form of tall tales; other times, they complimented me on my fresh face, my curly hair, "Shirley Temple—she'll be a heart-breaker." Sometimes they'd fight over which of them was going to marry me. Of course, it was pretend fight, for I'd seen pictures of Sergeant Nellie's blonde, German kid, like Dieter, and

Sergeant Dumkoski's German wife, who was fat like him. Each morning I fueled myself with their attentions. Sergeants Nellie and Dumkowski were not only fun, but made me believe that I mattered.

The civilian Tom lived on the fourth floor in many rooms, but he didn't come to meals. We rarely saw him, except as he left to walk Cecil, his black poodle, who yipped and ran away if anybody even looked at him. Each morning at 7:30 a.m., and each evening at 6:00 p.m., Tom, furled, black-striped umbrella in one hand and leash in the other, would nod at us immediately after Cecil's growl. Mother said he was a "bachelor," implying that this might be why he was "offish." Perhaps "bachelor" was a skin condition that made him not want to be seen. I felt sorry for him but was also a little scared. He was very pale, always wore a frown and walked too erectly.

One day, Tom fell and broke his leg. We didn't see much of him or Cecil after that, although he came downstairs sometimes on his crutches.

After a time, the Sergeants talked with my parents about something called "Korea" and being "deployed," whatever that meant. Each day one of the Sergeants seemed to get more excited about Korea.

I was getting fed up with no attention.

"What's Korea?" I asked.

"A country near China," Mommy answered.

"What does that have to do with us or with Germany?"

Both Sergeants laughed.

"Nothing, we hope, Little Girl," Sergeant Dumkowski belly laughed.

"Don't worry, the United States army will *always* protect you," Sergeant Nellie said.

I wasn't worried, and didn't like being called "Little Girl."

Then one day, the Sergeants weren't at breakfast. Neither was Daddy. Mother was reading the *Stars and Stripes* that Daddy usually read at breakfast. When I asked where the sergeants were, she explained they had been "reassigned." What did that mean? It meant that they would not be back. They would probably each go to Korea, although they would return to the USA first.

"Why didn't they say goodbye?" *Didn't I mean more to them? How could they leave like that, like a boy throwing a newspaper, then just disappearing?*

"I don't know, Honey; maybe they didn't have time." Mother folded her napkin, getting ready to leave the breakfast table. "Anyway, it will do them good to see their American wives at least once." Mommy curled her lip.

I couldn't believe my ears. "What?"

"It will be good for them to be in the U.S. and see their families. She put down the *Stars and Stripes* on the table. The headlines said something about "Dean Acheson, U.S. Secretary of State," making a speech.

"No! They're already married. Sergeant Dumkowski has a fat wife here! I've seen pictures of Sergeant Nellie's family; he has a kid who looks like Dieter."

***

Mother shook her head. "Each has a wife in the USA. I don't know about children or who has what." She gathered up the newspaper, making motions to leave.

"Then what will happen to the German wife, to Sergeant Nellie's child? Will they be left alone?"

"I don't know; they all do that." She paused and looked out at the back lawn. "Military men—maybe men in general."

"But it's wrong. Lying is wrong! You told me!"

"Yes, dear, but that's the way it is." She headed towards the stairs. "Maybe it's wartime—or maybe it's…. I don't know. I do know I need to wake up your father. He has a meeting at nine," she said, and up the stairs she clomped, shoulders sagging.

I went to a wing chair near the fireplace and sat in it, hidden and safe. Married? Both of them with wives here and in the USA? No, couldn't be; the Sergeants were American heroes. This accusation was bogus, like that first heart attack she had from imagining Jim staring at me on the outside staircase. Only I was certain neither sergeant had beaten up his mother with a tire iron. Such kind, frolicsome men would never commit such an offence. As for so-called army "orders," they explained nothing. Mommy had to be lying, *lying.* How could she? I hated her. So after a while, I went into the library and wouldn't come out for lunch or even dinner.

The following days held only the stomp of transient guests, the shuffling of my father down the stairs, and the thud of Tom's crutches. Only the patter of Cecil's paws animated the long days.

One day, I was curled up in a wing chair near the lounge reading when I heard voices.

"What have you done? *Again!* And in the entrance hall...god damn you! Idiot!"

Tom's crutches rat-a-tat tat, rat-a-tatted, like bullets.

"I'll have to pay a fortune after staff cleans up; *if* this carpet can be cleaned."

The back door creaked open—a haunted house groan.

"Why the devil do I put up with you? Stupid animal. Get out, do you hear! Get out!" A thud, a yelp, and then the sound of a door shut—slamming.

I huddled deeper into the chair. The stink of dog poop wafted from the hall. When Tom's crutches no longer sounded, I climbed down and went to the open back door.

On the back porch, Cecil lay with his face between his paws, legs tucked up under him like a child hiding under covers. Even his poodle curls seemed coiled under. I called his name and his tail moved slightly, but that was all. Gingerly, I approached and touched his head. Cecil glanced up; his eyes full of hopelessness and shame. He did not growl or run. "Poor doggie, poor doggie," I ventured a few pats; his curls bounced under my hand, mattress-like, and then began to stroke his neck. I was afraid he might bite, but didn't want to lose this opportunity. In my pocket was a jacks ball. I fished it out and rolled it towards him. He became instantly interested but didn't move. I grabbed the ball and tossed it about two feet from him. Cecil got up and went to it; we began a game of catch. After a while, the breeze got cold, so I got up and opened the door.

"Cecil?" I called. At his name, he shook himself. For a moment, he stared, then came trotting in, From then on Cecil and I were best friends; a bond even Daddy recognized and wrote to his mother in a letter postmarked July 4, 1950.

Cecil is a black French poodle belonging to Mr. Hitchman who lives at Ayer House. At first very aloof, Cecil has now developed a great friendship with Mary Hanford. They go almost everywhere together and make quite a striking pair.

***

The large clock, with the little people who danced on the hour, showed almost two hours had passed since Cecil and I had been on the back porch. It was nearly 5 p.m. Guilt overwhelmed me. Tom would be worried about his dog. I should take Cecil back, but Tom's aloofness scared me. His pale face seemed ghostly, and why would he want a whole floor to himself? Maybe he was a mad scientist, casting spells or making poisons or bombs. He probably had a gun hidden under his pillow. Was he even an American?

The sun was setting. Soon someone would close the drapes, signaling preparation for drinks, then dinner. In the lounge, Heinz was clinking bottles, lining them up, readying. Although Tom no longer walked Cecil, Tom would be wondering if someone had kidnapped his dog.

There was no remedying it: I had to take Cecil to the mysterious fourth floor and face Tom. I trudged up the stairs to the third floor, Cecil in my arms. By the time I reached the fourth floor, I was St. George bracing for battle with the dragon. But it was hard to knock with Cecil in my arms. I used my elbow to knock, but managed only a feeble sound. If I put the poodle down, he might run away. So I hauled back my right leg and kicked— bam!

"What the hell?" a voice from inside yelled. I kicked again. "For God's sake, come in!" Tom bellowed. "The door's open."

Why wasn't he answering the door himself? Was this a trick to shoot me with his gun? Well, if he did, he'd shoot his dog too, because I held him up in front of me.

Using my right elbow, I pressed down on the door lever. The door swung easily open and there, across the room, sat Tom in an ochre easy chair, one leg propped on a round leather ottoman. He was wearing a blue silk dressing gown over trousers, not pajamas. On an end table sat a tall highball glass and what looked like a thermometer.

"Pardon me, if I don't get up." Tom's mouth twisted. "Walking is now very painful." He pulled up a trouser leg to reveal a plaster cast.

"I've, I've brought back your dog," I stammered and put Cecil on the floor who ran and jumped on his lap. Tom winced, but then patted Cecil. "He was on the back porch."

"Damned dog! Well, don't stand there in the doorway, come in." Tom's pale face sagged, as he shifted slightly and picked up his drink. "Am obliged to you, I'm sure. Damn dog----Obviously, I can't chase after him." The frown etched like ink on his long face blurred; that face reminded me of a horse's face, the eyes also— big and sad. I glanced around. The large living room had a fireplace and also a bar. Beyond a half-open door I could see part of a bed.

"Can't even walk him now, much less run after him. At any rate, I'm much obliged." He quaffed his drink and using his arms lifted himself out of the wing chair, dumping Cecil on the floor.

"Don't have much appropriate for a little girl. Do have orange squash. Would you like some?" He started limping towards the bar, dragging a leg, Cecil circling him.

What was orange squash? Poison, like Nazis took instead of being captured by allies? The poor man was already leaning on the bar, alternating looking over it at me and wrinkling his face, muttering "bloody damn thing..." I had to go to the bathroom, but didn't dare ask. "Ouch, ow, god damn it!" Cecil was humping his leg. He kicked the poodle with his other leg, then sighed.

"Would you like me to walk Cecil now?" I asked. "It's past six."

"Leash over there," Tom jerked his head towards a coat tree near the door. On it hung a harness and leash, as well as a coat, umbrella and cane. I picked up the harness and leash. Cecil ran towards me. "No orange squash?"

"No, thank you," I replied, fastening the leash. "Too close to dinner. Come on, Cecil." I tugged on the lease.

"Hope you feel better," I said. As I closed the door, another thrill of triumph ran through me. I had exclusive possession of Cecil and had faced down the dragon who turned out not to be one, like the Wizard of Oz. As Cecil and I skipped down the stairs, I knew my lonely days were over. Now I just had to get Heinz to look after him temporarily, while I found a bathroom.

***

After a while, although I played mostly with Cecil, I took to visiting Tom who seemed endlessly crippled, but who at least talked to me, mainly about the war.

"Damn Brits think they're so superior. Why didn't they use the intelligence the Poles gave them five weeks before the war started? Could have saved millions of lives…. Maybe too stupid to understand it." Tom would rant, pull a blanket up around him and ask me to do something. "Mary Hanford, get me my pills; forgot them this morning. There's a good girl." If it wasn't pills, it was water or blanket or whiskey or something. I didn't mind. Then he'd get onto Chamberlain, about how he "dithered around" when he should have annihilated Hitler when he invaded Czechoslovakia. Panty-waist claimed Nazis will not go farther. If we play nice; then they'll play nice with us.' Tom stuck his nose in the air as if smelling something bad. "Oh, puleeze," he made his voice high, like a woman's, then bent over and sighed "No balls at all. Chamberlain had no balls."

"Why didn't they have balls? How did they get their Cricket matches going without balls?"

But Tom didn't answer, just turned red. "Sorry, sorry."

"For what?"

"Sorry I ever worked for the idiots. If you're not well-born, you're not good enough, even if, no—especially if—you're an American." He hiccupped and looked as though he were going to cry. "Oh never mind!" Tom snapped, almost to himself, and he went on to tell me how his tailor had gotten his measurements wrong.

After a while, I realized Tom was almost like Daddy. He drank, just not as much and went on rants about Allies, like Daddy went on rants about the pope. But it was a little different because Tom couldn't do anything else. He was really mad at the allies, didn't like how Germany was split into West and East.

"Giving the goddam Russians the breadbasket of the country. Does no one ever learn? They invaded *here*, the Rhur Valley, during the war, and they *still* want it, mark my words. We never should have internationalized it."

"Why did you?"

"I didn't, but *your* like did. Oh, well, it was 1948." He looked far off out of the window. "And you thought you were doing the right thing. Bloody 'right thing!'" He turned back to me. That made me mad. How could he blame me?

"Wait! I didn't do anything. I didn't even *know* about it; I was only eight. I didn't come to Germany until now, and I'm ten. And I only came because Daddy got a job."

"Damn straight. I know." He motioned for me to get him some crackers which he had behind the bar, and I did. "And a damn complicated job it is, Krupp, Krupp—his U-boats killed your American soldiers. That little Jewish girl, Anne Something-Or-Other, might be alive if not for Krupp—she died just before war was over. The child wrote, 'I still believe people are good at heart.' —can you believe it?" He looked as if he were going to cry again.

"Would you like me to walk Cecil now?" I would get the harness and leash. This is how I got away from Tom when he made me too sad.

***

So I began to spend more time in the library and in the lounge, when my parents were out which was almost always. I would go to the library and look for different books, but there weren't many that interested me, only *Caesar and His Gallic Wars.* Sometimes I would go to the lounge and talk with whomever showed up in the afternoon. Mostly only one or two people came, but that was better than nothing. The bartender, Heinz, began to expect me. After a while, Tom left and took Cecil. Since Heinz and I were getting to be friends, I took the news of Tom and Cecil's departure in stride and was only a little sad. Besides, people were always leaving. I was getting used to it.

"What orders do you have?" I asked as Tom climbed into the Mercedes that was to take him and Cecil away.

"Orders?" Tom pulled the plaid car blanket over him and Cecil who was in his lap. Even though his broken leg was mended, both his legs were so wasted, they looked like twigs. No wonder he was cold.

"Yes. Where is your next assignment?" I felt very sophisticated for asking.

But Tom didn't say anything, only smiled slightly; he put out his hand and touched me on the cheek.

"Pretty child," he almost sang it, like a sad song. Then he pulled his hand in real quick and said "Mach snell" to the driver and they roared off. Cecil poked his head out the window as they left and barked once at me.

***

So I began spending even more time with Heinz, who always seemed glad to see me. Heinz was tall and had a pale moon face, dark hair slicked back and always wore black, like a tuxedo. He always seemed as mild as his usual blank expression. Once Daddy said Heinz might have gone to a British school and been a professional before the war. Heinz spent the daylight hours washing and polishing glasses. When I was bored with reading, I would wander into the lounge and climb up on one of the bar stools that surrounded the horseshoe-shaped bar. Like the window seats and chairs around the four round tables in the lounge, it was brown leather, only it had brass thumbtack things making patterns in the leather bar walls. Heinz, inside the bar, like in a circle, would not only wash and polish but would order bottles of different liquor.

Heinz chatted with me, but never teased. He taught me that gin was made from juniper berries, bourbon from corn and vodka from potatoes. Sometimes he talked about his mother but not much. He also helped me with German words. "Danke" meant "Thank You," "Bitte" meant "You're welcome," but I got it confused with "bitter" and "bitters" which went with drinks.

After a while, he also let me come into the horseshoe-shaped bar. Behind the bar were lots of shelves with glasses, bottles but also shelves that people couldn't see. Heinz kept cartons of cigarettes on hidden shelves in the bar, some bottles of pills, and chocolate bars, Hersheys. I told him I worried about Mommy and about having no friends. Heinz told me his wife had left him during the war and how he did not know where she or their children were. "Both you and me," he would say, "are not so different. We are both prisoners."

At night, when business picked up, Heinz had no time for chitchat but built a structure of tall glasses and bottles on the bar, which hid me as I sat on a stool behind the bar. The guests didn't see me, and Heinz could mug faces at me. Mother and Daddy were nearly always gone until very late, so I stayed up until almost midnight asleep on the stool. One evening I toppled off the stool in sleep, and made a loud thud. Nothing happened to either one of us.

Behind my tower I watched people, although they were blurred because I had to look through the highball glasses. Mostly, soldiers drank and talked, often about "black market" cigarettes and dollars. The term "black" scared me, and I asked Heinz what "black market" meant. He said he didn't know, but I knew he did. Sometimes couples on the window seats kissed. Through the glass tower they looked weird: first, there were two shapes with space or light between, but no edges to the shapes. Then when they came together to kiss, they looked like multicolored soap bubbles merging into one blob.

One night, Sergeant Dumkowski came in with the other soldiers, and he had a German woman with him. After a while when everybody was laughing, he introduced the woman as his fiancé who would come with him to Chicago when he left Germany. But I knew that Sergeant Dumkowski had a wife and a baby in the U.S. and said so to Heinz.

"Things happen during war," Heinz said.

"But the war's over!"

He turned to clean the faucets on the bar's sink. "You don't want your 'safe place' discovered. Better to keep quiet on this."

My tower never was discovered, so I kept hiding behind it. It was fun looking through those glasses, like being in a carnival's fun house with mirrors that distort everything. Not only did lovers become blobs, but huge soldiers who tromped in, especially if they were muddy, expanded behind the tower. They became khaki-colored dust clouds, threatening a storm. Sometimes they were monsters invading somewhere, which they really were sometimes. Oddly, the storm fantasy materialized right there in Ayre House.

One evening, my parents ate dinner at the hotel. Then Mother went up to our rooms, and Daddy and I went and sat at a table in the bar. I had a book with me but must have dozed off because Daddy's loud voice woke me.

"Yes, we are *still* here five years after the war. And we may be here twenty years. Somebody has to re-civilize this damn place." Daddy was sitting on a bar stool at the bar, frowning at Heinz. There was no one else there. I left the table and went to the bar but Daddy didn't notice. He was peering into his almost-empty glass.

"Would you like another double, Mr. Baldy?" Heinz's face twitched, as I crouched behind the tower of glasses.

Daddy grabbed the drink. Through the stack of glasses, his hand was magnified—a Goliath hand with massive thumbs. "You Germans think you are so damn smart. Your Ayrian master-race theory should have tipped some of you off." He threw his head back and laughed. "You really thought you could get away with it?"

I hunkered down to peer through the first row of glasses. The first row had the most glasses; it not only magnified but produced a prism effect. Daddy's head was huge; lights bounced off his glasses, his pearl cuff-links glistened. Through cut glass, he seemed fragmented, shot through with colored lights.

"Let me tell you—we are going to uncover and take every arsenal, every asset, and every remnant of post-war Reich2."

He thrust his glass towards Heinz, which Heinz filled and then moved back a little. Daddy bolted the whiskey and began to recount Germany's defeat, stage by stage, from the initial Polish conquest to Hitler's suicide and a note. Daddy was going slowly to get Heinz worked up, to rub it in.

Right after he talked about the note, he launched into the country's guilt, Heinz's guilt. "But you didn't need Hitler's note about Jews, did you? Now all of you say you didn't know, that you feel guilt now that you know. How could you *not* know what was happening? Why were those cattle cars filled with people? Railroads here are everywhere." Daddy swayed a bit on the stool, half closed his eyes. I was scared. Would Daddy come round the bar and get Heinz? What would he do when he found me?

Then three soldiers strode into the bar laughing about something. I heard them plop down at a table but paid no attention to us. I could tell that they were tall and big but the glass blurred the rank insignia on their uniforms. One of them signaled to Heinz.

"Hey, Herr WhosIt."

Daddy's voice got even louder.

"You followed a demented, evil man— 'Heil, Hitler.' You crowed with bloodlust. You! Don't pretend you didn't," Daddy thudded his glass on the bar. "All of you should have been obliterated, bombed to smithereens, like the japs! Germans so stupid with their idiotic philosophy of a super-race. If anybody has a super-race. It is us, the Americans. Doesn't your soul curl when you think of what you did? Don't you smell those people burning?" Daddy patted the bar. "And is this leather bar made of

Jew skin, Heinz? Did you skin and stretch it over boards to make it serviceable?"

"That's enough," Heinz said. His low voice rumbled, and he looked very, very mad. "You think we are cowed," muttered Heinz, "by being occupied by Americans, British and French. Did it ever occur to you that you, yes, *you* set us up for the Reich by your punishing Versailles Treaty?" Heinz came from behind the bar and towards Daddy; his face tree-toad white, his hands doubled. "Revenge begets revenge. I'm an educated man and know we will come back."

One of the GIs stood up from the table. "Problem, Mr. Baldy? Need a little help with this Kraut?" When I heard their chairs scrape, I ran, toppling the glass tower into tinkling shards and hid behind one of the lobby's drapes. Paralyzed with fear, I listened to loud voices and stuff being knocked over. I waited for Daddy to come out, but he didn't. Nobody did.

Upstairs, my parents' room was unlocked. Mother was snoring softly when I curled up beside her and thought about Heinz, Mommy was warm and the room was dark; she was the only one who had not left, in one way or the other.

The next day Heinz was not at work, and I didn't see Daddy at all. The next few days someone else was always tending bar. That week when Mommy finally came back for dinner at Ayre House, she said "our house" was ready. We were going to move into a huge, wonderful place and have maids, so although it would be hard for me to adjust, I would love it! She was wrong; it wouldn't be hard to adjust. The only hard part about leaving Ayre House would be remembering Cecil, his head out the Mercedes window, his last bark. Cecil left me too, but he didn't have a choice.

We moved out of Ayre House first into a temporary house until our assigned house was ready. The semi-circle of a room that jutted out into the front lawn became the family "den" and was where my parents had cocktails. Each twilight the chiming of the city bells at 6 p.m. announced supper. Then I would eat delicious leftovers from a meal when my parents were home, in the immense paneled dining room and read Cowboy and Indian books at first, then later mysteries. This solitary dinner was always a privilege because Mommy wouldn't let me read at the table when they were home. When they were home, I just had to sit there, twitching with boredom and trying not to show it while they, usually Daddy, went on and on about McCloy, Alfried, the Pope, Truman, MacArthur and about "policy." I knew Truman was the president. Afried, I had a hunch, was a Krupp who once lived at Villa Hugel and whom Daddy was supposed to "disable." The pope was a little, skinny man who wore white. I'd seen him on television.

So, I began to wonder about the conversations, what the point was. One time I asked Mommy why Krupp was such a big deal. She said he was very rich and had to turn over his money to the allies, which seemed odd to me.

"What did he do?" I asked.

Mommy, who was reaching for a spice in a high-up kitchen cabinet, said, "Krupp's money built the Autobahn." The Autobahn was a nice, smooth highway that got us places easier than the little, bumpy roads.

"What's wrong with that?"

She brought down a box of nutmeg, then turned to me with a frown and scrunched eyes. "Hitler!" Her voice pitched higher on the "ler," as if in warning or I should have known better.

But I didn't connect that Hitler had built the Autobahn for his troops, nor had it soaked in that Krupp had financed the war, even though I'd more or less been told. All I knew was that Mommy's tone scared me. I still thought the Autobahn an improvement, but didn't ask her any more about Krupp. Judging from Villa Hugel's splendor, Krupp must have had a lot of money, so perhaps he could make trouble. It didn't seem likely, though, now that the allies were living in his house. After all, the war was over.

Chapter Three

Classified Information

We lived for a while in a house where the poor owner lived in the basement but only until our permanent house became available. It didn't seem worth the chaos to move but we did because it was a very grand house. Still it was silly, as nothing could be grander than Villa Hugel, so what was the point?

Seven Elasse Strasse was supposedly two-story but really four floors including the basement and the top floor. In the back, giant woods guarded the back yard and mulberry bushes. Off the dining room snuggled a place called a Winter Garden, a room made almost entirely of glass and filled with plants. I loved the light and the way the air smelled moist and green. Tucked into my compact bedroom was a cozy built-in bed with drawers where I could hide. It also sported a balcony with a railing, like our Frankfurt hotel room, but was really the rooftop of the round room. I could step outside on it and look over Essen and Heisingen. In the black-and-white diagonally tiled bathroom upstairs a weird toilet whooshed. Mommy called it a Water Closet, and the small tub that squirted out water where I bathed my dolls a Bidet.

I had already been in the basement before Mommy forbade me. Down there was a huge wringer washer, and a small room off to the side of the main room. That tiny room had a thick door and a tiny square window with bars. It looked like a cell.

"Mommy," I asked, "who did the Germans put in that jail cell downstairs?"

"What jail cell?"

"You know, that little room in the basement."

"You are *not* to go into the basement."

"I know that now, but I went before you told me. So, who stayed in the jail?"

Mommy took a deep breath, then said kind of loud, "I don't know that it is a jail. Any information like that would be classified. Even if it weren't classified, I'd just as soon not know." She shook her head.

"But isn't Seven Elasse Strasse classified already as a house? What else would it be?"

"Oh, Baby, you are so literal." She hugged me. "The word *classified* in the way I'm using it means *secret*. Our government wants to keep certain information secret. It's better for us not to know."

"Why? You always tell me to tell you everything."

She released me and turned a bit away. "Well, sometimes governments have to make hard choices, so it's better that not everything is known."

I thought all choices were hard. "But if the people are the government as Daddy says, why would our government keep secrets from the people?"

"Sometimes those hard choices involve hurting someone in order not to hurt everyone. Information management is for the good of all." Mommy's chin drooped

"So someone ended up in the basement jail so as not to hurt everyone?"

"Oh, Mary Hanford, I can't explain everything! Just stay out of there; you might trip and fall, and no one would hear you."

"No, I wouldn't." Did she still think I was a baby?

"No arguing. I've had enough."

When she got that tone, there was nothing more I could do. Maybe she didn't want me to realize that every kid was in a jail, prisoner of his parents and almost any adult.

So I dropped the basement subject and asked about the attic where I had not been. Mommy wasn't so harsh about the attic. She sat down on the yellow chaise lounge in the bedroom. Her face took on a teacher look, and she said there were two reasons I wasn't to go into the attic.

"The first reason is that the attic isn't finished, so you might get hurt. The lighting is not good, and you might trip or something.

The second reason, Mary Hanford, that you should stay out of the attic is that despite not being finished, the attic will be the maids' quarters, their home. That floor will belong to whomever I hire, and none of us is to intrude on them. Do you understand?"

"Not really."

"Would you like anyone just crashing into this home?"

"No."

"The servants will be around us working every day and have to do what your father and I say. They deserve the dignity of privacy after their work is done."

I wasn't sure what "dignity of privacy" meant but did know the need for escape.

"You mean like having my own room?"

"Precisely."

"Okay." Dignity of privacy sounded important, and I didn't want to ruin it. I pictured a young woman making a single bed with hospital corners and an older grandma-type crocheting doilies for their tables without anyone bossing them around.

***

We hadn't even gotten all the boxes open when people from Villa Hugel, mostly American and English and some French people, visited. Essen was in the British sector and Frankfurt in the American sector. I never went to the Russian sector and was only in the French section once.

The first Americans, the Forquins, were loud. They just showed up. When Mommy opened the door, Mrs. Forquin sang "If I knew you were coming, I'd have baked a cake," and thrust out a cake at her. This was strange because according to the song, Mommy was the one who should have baked the cake.

Mrs. Forquin invited me to their daughter Sondra's third birthday party the next day. They told us that their German Sheppard had rescued their daughter Sondra when she fell into a pool, but I didn't believe them. First, a dog couldn't do that. Second, why would a German dog rescue an American child?

But when I saw the German Sheppard at their ornate German house, I began to believe it might have rescued Sondra. Although all it did was lie around, its eyes looked kind of wild when someone got near Sondra. Since Sondra was turning three, all the other kids were younger than me and didn't say "please" or "thank you." I couldn't tell if that was because they were so young or that no one had taught them. It was just a little kid party, except for a crepe paper animal hung up from the ceiling in the living room. It looked like a giraffe but it was made of lots of colors. That lifted it out of the ordinary. I thought it was neat, until I found out everyone had to hit it with a stick until it broke. So we lined up and all took a swack out at it. When it broke, candy came out of it, and everyone rushed to get the candy. Even though I played, it was wrong to teach little kids to hit things, especially animals. I'll bet they wouldn't try that with the German Sheppard. Besides, my dress was stiff and made red marks on me.

The British people who visited didn't just show up, but always called ahead. They spoke English like rat-a-tat-rat and were polite, to the point of being fake but at least they didn't thrust cake at us. Most of their kids went to a school just for British, and some went to a school that had "board." This sounded awful until I found out that "board" only meant students slept at the school, which was pretty strange.

A British woman, Mrs. Merrilees, visited Mommy with her daughter Dawn. Mrs. Merrilees had mixed blonde and grey hair, half-and-half. She wore high-necked dark dresses and a pendant watch that dangled over a cliff-like chest which seemed to thrust her forward. She could have been a pigeon but her legs were too long. Mrs. Merrilees promoted all things British. Her daughter Dawn had freckles, a Buster Brown haircut, and wore very nice clothes. She sat quietly next to her mother, hands folded. Then when Mrs. Merrilees and Mommy were talking a lot, Dawn leaned towards me.

"You know, American or not, I could walk over and play sometime. You have a very nice house, after all," Dawn almost whispered. I didn't like the way Dawn sounded. "And then perhaps we could ride."

"Ride? What?"

"Don't you ride?" I shook my head.

"Oh." Dawn sniffed and didn't say anything more.

Mrs. Merrilees and Mommy visited a lot. Most of the time we called on them. Often Dawn and I didn't play long, because she had riding lessons, elocution lessons, violin lessons, decorum lessons and French. Besides, Dawn was a brat. If she were at my house and didn't get her way, she'd threaten to leave and I'd give in because I didn't have other friends. She did other stuff too, like lauding it over me because she had privileged information. Her secrets made me feel even more like an outsider. Eventually I got mad and when the driver picked us up to take us to some Villa Hugel tea that was to include family, I tried to have privileged information too.

For the tea, Dawn wore grey, nubby knee socks which went with her grey and brown plaid skirt and a shiny blouse which went with her shiny brown hair. I was not that well turned out because Mommy was already at Villa Hugel, so couldn't supervise. I had thrown on that scratchy yellow dress I wore to Sondra's party, but which hadn't been cleaned or ironed. I hadn't brushed the knots out of my hair, nor washed my face. It didn't need washing. Besides, I didn't care, for I finally knew something Dawn didn't. I knew about Mrs. Glass's baby and intended to show Dawn up. I'd practiced in the mirror how to look when you've got a secret. Mouth curved, head back a little.

Dawn's green eyes were already glittering—she was waiting to be mean. So I curved up my mouth but said nothing. Bump, squish, went the car. The wind yelled or maybe it was the sound of the engine.

"What are you smiling about?" Dawn nudged my foot.

"Oh, nothing." Outside, the hard rain pelted the car's roof hard, like bullets shooting.

"Yes, something!"

"Oh, just that I learned something—but it's a secret." We lurched around a curve so fast that I fell a little. Dawn clutched her coat.

"Secret? Well, we mustn't spill a secret, must we?" Dawn stared like she was going to kill me. But I didn't *say anything*. She fished a book out of her satchel and pretended to read, but I knew she felt bad because I knew something she didn't. She never moved with the jolts, just kept looking at the book, head down, hair flopping over her face. But I could see some face; it was really white, car-sick white. Maybe I had upset her too much; maybe I'd made her sick. My stomach twisted.

"Mrs. Glass is going to have a baby," I said. But I didn't tell her that this was the secret.

"So, that's it!" Dawn looked up, her cheeks were getting red fast. She didn't look sick at all.

"What's 'it'?" The Mercedes pulled up to the entrance. I could see the great hall all lit up, even though it wasn't really dark.

"The secret."

"No, it isn't." I wished I had brushed my hair, so started fumbling for a comb in my pocket. There was no comb.

"Stupid! You'd fall for anything. What's that word you Americans use? Sucker?" Slamming her book shut, she tossed it aside and skipped out of the car.

***

Once the visitors had gone and we had eaten all their cakes and unpacked boxes, Mommy had to hire help for the house. It was her part of Daddy's job—again—Villa Hugel flowing outside. I would get up in the morning and see her in the kitchen all dressed up, talking to German women. Sweat misted her brow and her shoulders hunched. Her nervousness made no sense to me, because she was going to now have help. It never occurred to me that she didn't know German and had to interview people who didn't speak English.

Mother finally hired Emmy, who was tall, stick-skinny with sallow skin and a large hook nose who spoke English. She also hired Hannahlore, a dumpy blonde with a kind expression. I could imagine myself crawling into her lap and cuddling up against her substantial bosom. She said Daddy was to hire the outside help, so he did.

Daddy hired Albert, the furnace man, and Herr Prusnat, a gardener. Albert was to bring us coke, not the drink, but dried-up coal. Then he was to load it into the basement, check the furnace and keep it going. This seemed to be a big deal at Villa Hugel's Coal Commission where Daddy worked. From what I could tell, the Coal Commission was to keep everyone from freezing because there wasn't enough fuel to go around. Albert scared me because of the permanent grime in his fingers and in his seamed face. Those lines reminded me of Jim, the man who freaked Mommy out because he beat up his mother with a tire iron.

Herr Prusnat was to be gardener and handyman. Herr Prusnat had been an American POW and had good recommendations. Herr Prusnat seemed like any other German, brown hair, blue eyes, only older. He could have even been thirty. He was quiet until you got to know him. If you asked him about the war, he would usually just say the Americans were good to him.

Mommy had declared Emmy as head housekeeper because she spoke English and because she thought she'd be competent, and she was right. Emmy was an eagle ready to swoop down and clutch at any sign of disorder. Her large eyes glinted savagely; her clipped English was brusque, her stride long and manly, and her energy endless.

Every evening at six, clatter, clatter, clack went the wooden shades as she lowered them. Every afternoon at four, cucumber sandwiches and tea would appear at my place in the parlor. From the kitchen wafted smells of strudel, roasts and cabbage. Dinner was at nine, Emmy serving in starched ruffled bib apron, and Hannahlore clearing up and from what I heard later from the kitchen's clank and clink cleaning up. Promptly, at 10:30, if I were awake, I would hear Hannahlore padding upstairs, usually with more laundry, mostly linens upstairs to where they lived on the third floor.

Sometimes I would wake to the smells of bread, coffee or cakes and go to the kitchen to get some of what was baking. Then I would sit with the house people because it was warm, but I didn't understand anything they said and the room was really dark. After I had eaten sometimes I drifted into the folding room, next to the kitchen where I could still hear them and there were two windows. In the folding room were two long tables, laundry supplies and an ironing board. Once I poked around and found a stash of soap scraps, hidden behind clothespins; it didn't take Nancy Drew to figure out someone was sneaking them to a family.

Living at Seven Elasse Str. seemed to require my parents to go out of town a lot. One of the weekends they were away, a swaggering, jolly two-year-old, Manfried, appeared. When I came into the kitchen, Manfried narrowed his eyes and planted his chubby legs firmly next to Hannahlore. Albert huddled in his black jacket and hovering over a cup of coffee eyed me with his usual glowering expression, yet he lit up when Manfried toddled past and touched Manfried's hair with an angel's tenderness. When I asked Hannahlore to come with me to my room, and she began to leave, Manfried yowled and grasped her around the legs. He was cute but pushy.

One morning, Mother came home early. Manfried heard the front door creak open and set up a howl.

"Good Lord, what is that?" Mommy ran into the kitchen. "Well!"

Manfried scooted behind Hannahlore's back and hid. Hannahlore looked down and twisted her apron, hunched over a little, as if someone was going to hit her.

"Who is this? Emmy?"

"Das es Manfried, Hannahlore's son. Her childcare was not available today. I was certain that Madam would not wish the boy to stay alone, so I gave permission."

"Oh, of course." Relief flooded Mommy's face.

"The boy is angry because he could not obtain a cookie. Perhaps you will allow me to give him one?" Emmy's tone reminded me of a weather report. Her face smooth and imperturbable.

"Cookie? Give him one, or more, or the whole box!" she laughed. Manfried peered out from behind Hannelore's skirt. "You be the judge, Emmy, I have to unpack. Mr. Baldy will be here for dinner, Emmy. Let's have—oh, I don't know what we have…"

"May I suggest sauerbraten, Madam?" Emmy had been marinating the meat for sauerbraten ever since my parents left.

Suddenly, I realized what Nancy Drew would have known at once, Emmy was an ex-Nazi! She was too frightening and slick to be anything else. Emmy ran the house like a squadron preparing a sneak attack, silently, without incident but with total victory. She could command a household, a neighborhood, a battalion, a world. Emmy had probably been a member of the *S.S.*, which was kind of a super Nazi. Maybe *S.S.* stood for "Super Stealth." *Help.* I thought. *Help.*

"Wonderful, Emmy. Now I must unpack." She bent down, kissed me and left the kitchen. I followed her.

As she unpacked, I listened to Mommy talk about her trip and helped her hang up her clothes. Now that Manfried was introduced, I asked where Manfried's father was, but she just sighed and shrugged her shoulders.

"You mean you don't know? Do you think it's Albert? Are they married?"

"Oh, just hush, Mary Hanford." So I did.

***

After Manfried's discovery, Hannahlore kept her head down, was extra quiet, and sometimes sad looking. Although she'd been hired as a general purpose maid, laundry was her obsession. She was constantly bringing sheets or towels down to the gigantic basement wringer washer, or carrying ironed, folded stacks upstairs. The stacks were in rectangles, squares, diagonal, even star or polygon shapes. Except for the laundry stacks and dust and dirt disappearing in her wake. She seemed like a piece of the furniture.

She was the kind who would always eat potatoes even when she didn't have to.

One night, when Mommy and Daddy were gone, I woke up late with a churning stomach. I vomited again and again, so I was scared my whole stomach would come up through my mouth and land in the toilet. Putting my hand over mouth, I tiptoed up to the third floor and burst in, hoping to wake them up.

But both of them were awake, even very late at night. Emmy was darning, and Hannahlore was in a nook bending over a large basket, presumably the clean laundry basket. The attic was grimy and black. There was no ceiling, only dirty rafters with occasional cobwebs that they must have missed. From the ceiling hung one bare light bulb. There were two cot-like beds covered with clean but ratty comforters, two straight chairs, and a rocker with slats, a couple missing, in the back. The attic was warm, though, cozy warm.

***

"I threw up three times." I pointed to my stomach. Emmy put down her sewing, one of Daddy's socks with a huge hole pulled over something. "What's that in the sock?"

"Let's go, *Du*." And she took my hand. In the kitchen, she boiled water, then put something in it and made me drink. It settled my stomach. Then we climbed back to that blackened room.

"Sittenez plaz." Emmy sat in the rocker and pointed to her lap, and I crawled into it. "'Vas es los?' You ask what happens to Papa's sock? Es 'darning egg.'" That's what she called what Daddy's sock was stretched over, and that's what it looked like, an egg made out of china—white also. The hole was so big, we would have just thrown the sock away, but Emmy was weaving over it with thread; it was kind of like making a pot-holder in camp.

"How can you fill up the hole like that? And it's late to be working."

"Much vork." She shook her head. It was hard for her to darn with me in her lap. "But gut Vork is gut; vork saves." Emmy began to rock a little. Even though Emmy's lap was bony, but nice and warm, I felt myself slipping into sleep.

Then a sudden shriek startled me awake.

"Shush, shoosh…" Hannahlore whispered. Then another cry. In the dim light, I could make out Hannahlore bending and picking up Manfried bundled in layers and layers—Manfried—the source of Hannahlore's laundry obsession.

"It is a secret, Poodle, not to tell." Emmy smoothed my hair and began to hum, then sing softly.

"You mean it's classified?"

"Classified? Vat you know about classified?" She began soft, rolling laughter that lasted a while, but I don't know how long because I drifted off. In the morning, I woke in my own bed.

I remembered that Emmy had told me to hush up about Manfried. So I did. But keeping it from Mommy wasn't easy. When Mommy stayed home, I rejoiced. During nice weather I often hid in the mulberry bushes and made up stories. Mommy once brought out watercress sandwiches on white rounds of breads and I'd pretended to share them with wood nymphs. That evening I told her my stories. Whatever we did, the hours we spent together glowed. They reminded me when she would pick me up at Collegiate School, or take me to piano lessons. When she was home, her smile was like the smile when I won the silver dollars for a piano contest. I wanted that smile more than anything.

Of course, I didn't tell Mommy I had classified information from friends because that would make her mad. There seemed no way out of that box, so one time I tested Mommy.

The test involved Dawn's secret, which I had sworn to keep. When Mommy pushed me so hard to tell her everything, I decided that she, of all people, was trustworthy. Didn't husbands tell secrets to their wives? I was pretty sure Daddy told Mommy Villa Hugel stuff. They told their wives because their wives were supposed to be part of them. I was really part of Mommy because I had come out of her stomach.

"Dawn told me a secret, one I mustn't tell anyone."

Mommy cuddled me closer. "Of course, I won't tell, Darling."

"Dawn has worms."

"Worms!" Her eyelids fluttered

"Yes." *Uh oh.*

"You know, Honey, her mother really should know about this."

My stomach dropped. *She's going to tell Dawn's mother and Dawn will know I betrayed her.* Mommy failed the test, and I learned why some things were classified.

We hadn't been moved in long when Mommy and Daddy began to talk about a car. We'd never had a car; now it seemed that we could. Daddy had to pick up a car in Bremen, another city. But Daddy didn't drive; so someone else had to drive him—Herr Prusnat. Their talk went on and on. Then for a couple days Daddy wasn't home. Mommy went about stuff and I read, as it had gotten colder, so I couldn't play outside.

Daddy got home before lunch on a cold, dismal day.

"Frances, Frances, I'm home." She didn't answer. Daddy went into the round room and poured himself a drink from the bottles which stood on the tea-table. Then he pulled a curtain-like big ring at the end of a ribbon which made a sound in the kitchen. Emmy strode in the round room and stood, hands folded.

"Where is Mrs. Baldy?" He frowned as if Mommy's not being home was Emmy's fault.

"I do not know, Herr Baldy." Emmy stood like she had a steel stick in her spine. I stood there too, afraid Emmy would get yelled at, but she didn't.

"That's all," Daddy sniffed.

"Would Herr Baldy require anything else?" He shook his head. When she went back into the kitchen I went upstairs.

When Mommy came home about four, Daddy began to yell at her. I ran downstairs into the round room to help, but Mommy turned out her palm towards me. "Mommy!"

"It's all right. You father wants to make a fuss because I wasn't home when he got back with the car, although how I'd know when he would arrive is beyond me." She panted a little, her bosoms heaved.

"Damn right I'm going to make a fuss." Daddy began a yelling rant that went on and on.

I felt bad for Mommy, but there was nothing I could do. Nothing, ever, no matter how much I wanted to change things. I tiptoed back upstairs. I had sneaked a bag of potato chips from Mommy's commissary stash, so ate them and just hid under the covers. I don't know what happened to dinner, as no one came to get me. Daddy went to sleep by 8:30, but not before I heard Mommy crying. When I heard him snoring, went downstairs. She was in the dining room writing letters.

"Who are you writing, Mommy?"

"My father, Sweetheart, your granddaddy." She didn't look up.

"May I write him too?"

"Sure." She passed me a piece of stationary. So I sat beside her and wrote Granddaddy too. I told him about the bombed buildings and about our beautiful house. I asked him how the goldfish were in his pond and did the study where he wrote his sermons still smell like cigars? That last part made me laugh, because I'd never told him his study stank. By the time Mommy and I were finished with our letters, we both felt better. At least I hope she did, because she didn't say anything, just stuffed our letters into one envelope, licked the sealing part and kissed me goodnight. The next morning I felt as if I'd been in a bad rainstorm in which the flowers were not dead, but pelted down, and I couldn't stop it.

"Mommy, last night felt like I was in a nightmare, but I wasn't. It was like I was outside in a storm that almost killed the flowers, but not quite. The worst part was there wasn't anything I could do to save anything."

"Honey, nobody can stop rain or flowers from being killed by rain. It's up to God."

"I know," I sighed.

"Then why did you bring it up?"

About a week later, Mommy came to my room after I'd gone to bed. Her face was splotched red and white and her glasses spotty. When she sat on my bed, I pulled up the covers because I was cold all of a sudden.

"You know your grandfather was more than a Methodist minister. He was handy. He made a wooden swing for me when I was very little. And he wasn't afraid to stand up to pressure. He bought me a white linen dress for graduation, even though the elders thought it an extravagance."

"What's an extravagance?"

"Too much money to spend on something."

"Oh."

"And he told everybody he wanted me to go to college, even though I was a girl."

She dabbed at her eyes with a washcloth she had brought from the bathroom and began another story, and I got bored.

"Yes, I know Granddaddy is nice. Remember when I fell in the fishpond? You had told me not to go, but not only did I go, I fell in!"

Mommy nodded and then let out a tiny laugh. "Yes, I was furious. Your grandfather talked me out of punishing you."

"He said, 'So you've never disobeyed, Frances,' and he chuckled. Then he said, 'I and you know better.' And I knew he was right."

"So we both know he was good. Why are you talking about it?"

Mommy hiccupped and waved a crumpled piece of paper at me. "Because he's dead. My daddy is dead."

"Why?" I began to cry.

"He was seventy-five; he was old. When people get old, they die." Mommy choked, letting tears flow, wiping them away with a monogrammed hanky.

"He never even got my letter. He never got my letter." I sobbed. The more I thought about Granddaddy's dying, the worse I felt. Mommy said it was okay because Granddaddy knew I had written him and that was all that counted. But how could he have known? There hadn't been time enough for our letters to arrive and both of them were in one envelope. Again, I couldn't make anything better.

After Granddaddy died, I began to pull at my nails until they bled and then drip the blood on Raggedy Ann's candy heart. Somehow, but I don't know how—it was like if I bled, other things wouldn't hurt me or maybe even other people so much. It was the start of something I did from then on—not drip onto a doll—but tear at my cuticles. Mommy hated it, and finally put medicine on my fingers that tasted bad that was supposed to make me stop but didn't. Nothing changed, until the Indian came.

The Indian was very tall with black hair and a few feathers in his hair, not a chief. He wore clothes though, clothes with fringe. He would creep quietly up the stairs in his moccasins after I had gone to bed and stand by the bed. Just as I was about to fall asleep, he'd tucked me in. Sometimes, he'd run some feathers over my face, so light and cool they were. It was as if to say I'll keep watch for you. You can go to sleep now. It's safe. He must have had an eagle as his power totem.

The Indian always came just as I was about to fall asleep but not quite. So when he came and ran his feathers over me, I dropped off into a deep, wonderful sleep. After a while, I began to count on the Indian and would hear his soft footsteps on the stairs—even though no one else could or ever knew he was there. After that, when I began to count on his coming, I stopped tearing at my nails. Mommy noticed my nails weren't bloody any more, but I never told her why.

Days at Elasse Strasse were boring. At Ayre House people were always coming and going. Even if they didn't speak to me, something was happening, even if it was just the staff arguing. A grown-up told Mommy to give me the Sears Catalog; that the Sears Catalog kept her kids amused for hours. So, I got one and looked through all the pages. But what good was it if you couldn't actually get any of the stuff? Mommy said I could but that it would take a long time to ship them to Essen. So I just looked and looked until I finally had it almost memorized.

One time, a British woman visiting Mommy asked me if I "did horses."

"What?" I said and remembered that Dawn had asked the same question.

So every Saturday I went to a ring and took horseback riding lessons. I got to wear a special outfit, a black cap but with chin straps and black pants with poufy things on the sides. Although I was a beginner, I felt important, that I could go places, not just on a horse, but in life. I thought I'd see Dawn there, but the teacher told me she was in the Advanced Class.

I didn't have any trouble getting on and off a horse and walking him, but that wasn't enough. The teacher, a big blonde British woman wanted me to post. Post meant going up and down in stirrups when the horse was trotting, only when he was trotting. When the horse raised his foot, I had to stand up and then get quickly down, so the horse could trot right. But I couldn't do it; I was always "off rhythm" as the riding teacher said. Her voice got more and more clipped.

"Straight now! Carry on. Blimey—this is a *simple* thing. Post up, post down." The teacher yelled, but I just couldn't get it. It was sort of like trying to get a tap dance rhythm, which I never got either. After a few Saturdays, I asked Mrs. Forquin if Americans rode differently in a way that they didn't have to post.

"Oh, you mean Western style," she answered. "Western style doesn't use posting, and it has a different saddle."

That next Saturday I asked the teacher if I could ride Western style.

"Good God! So now we have Americans wanting to be cowboys as well as victors, do we? Sorry, British standards here!" She yell-laughed. So that was the end of that.

I kept trying; and almost learned to post, but not quite. Teacher didn't give up on me but I gave up on myself because of a substitute horse. I don't know what happened, but that horse started to cantor when I wanted it to trot. I yelled "Whoa" real loud and dug my heels into him. He finally stopped, but not until after he had left the ring and was cantering in the field. Then I realized that the horse, or any horse, could run away with me. I'd seen a movie where a little girl was thrown off a horse and killed. Suddenly, I felt as if I had already been knocked down, as I couldn't get my breath. I would never learn to post and that posting seemed the only thing that counted. So I told Mommy I didn't want any more lessons, but kept the reason classified. I didn't want to scare her.

It was after the move, riding lessons and Granddaddy's death that I missed Cecil the most. Then I missed him so much I ached. Cecil would have loved to romp in these beautiful lawns, even nicer than that at Ayre House. One morning, when Daddy was at Villa Hugel, I went to Mommy.

"Mommy, there's nothing to do and I miss Cecil. I miss him so much that I get a headache. I want a dog. Can I have dog?" I told her that ever since I petted Tiny Bits' blonde cocker spaniel, I had yearned for a dog like hers.

"Tiny Bits! But you were only four. How can you remember her, much less her dog?"

"Tiny bits had a blonde cocker spaniel, bright yellow pencils and a box of over a hundred crayons and wore a red jacket. That jacket had a pointy hood."

"Mercy!" She looked far off. "We'll think about a dog, but you'll have to take care of it, if it happens."

I waited, but nothing happened. I forgot about it until like I did everything else that didn't happen, until one night Daddy told me about his collie, Donald. I never knew he'd ever had a dog.

"Donald was my best friend, and I was good for him. I brushed his long brown and white hair every day and made sure he always had fresh water. We went for long walks. No matter what happened, I always knew Donald would be my friend." He reached for his martini glass, finished his drink, and then held it out to Mommy to make him another.

"We're out of olives," Mommy said.

"Just make the damn drink," he said. So she did.

"One summer, I had to go to my grandfather's plantation. There was work to do, and he needed someone to supervise, as he had hurt his leg. The workers knew and liked me. Grandfather Henderson seemed to think they would take directions from a teenager they knew better than from a man he hired. And I guess they did. So I went and stayed the whole summer. When I came back home to start school, Donald was gone." He gulped his drink, so there was only a sliver of liquid left in the shallow triangular glass.

"Gone? How could he be gone? Where?"

"Just gone, Mary Hanford. I asked my parents about Donald, but no one told me. I never found out." He sounded like a child who'd been hit but wouldn't cry. Indignation rose in me.

"But they had to explain, didn't they? That's terrible. It makes no sense."

"A lot of things don't make sense, Mary Hanford. Why was there another World War? Why did the Germans let Hitler rise to power; why didn't we enter the war sooner? For all our cant about freedom, we dodged what was happening in Europe until Pearl Harbor." He slumped back into his easy chair. "And why are we now squabbling with the goddam French?"

I didn't know what cant meant or why we were squabbling with the French, but I did know Daddy was getting off the subject. I also knew that Daddy should have protested when his dog disappeared.

"Did you ask your parents again and again what happened to Donald?"

"No, Mary Hanford. I did not." His eyelids drooped.

"Why not?"

Daddy didn't answer. Instead his head fell forward onto his chest, and he breathed heavily. He was fast asleep right there.

"Run along, Honey. I'll get Daddy up to bed," Mommy said. So I did.

After that, I heard nothing more about Donald. I tried not to think about Cecil and most of the time, I didn't. Then one evening, before dinner, Mommy came to me and Daddy had gone to Weisbaden to get my dog.

"We had to research it. And, Honey, this puppy is not a Cocker Spaniel, but a Springer Spaniel with very, very smart parents. They both have papers to prove it. We would have gotten him sooner but they wouldn't let him go until he was six weeks old," Mommy said, her face softening, as if she were thinking of a baby. "And oh, he is black, not blond."

Why would the dog's parents have papers; weren't they already housebroken? And what was Weisbaden, a town? Why didn't they ask me about having a Springer Spaniel instead of a Cocker one? Why black?"

"Where is Weisbaden? How did Daddy get there?"

"In our car, Sweetheart."

"In the Chevrolet? The one from Bremen?"

"Of course." Her laugh tinkled like bells. She seemed to have forgotten the row when Daddy came back from Bremen.

"Herr Prusnat drove him?"

"Yes."

Then it was okay. Herr Prusnat was nice. Although he didn't speak English, he always tousled my curls and warned me if I was about to step on something sharp in the yard. Once when I saw a slug and went screaming towards the house, Herr Prusnat was the only one who didn't laugh at me.

"Oh, Mommy, thank you, thank you!" I flung my arms around her.

That evening Joey came home. When I took him out of his cage, he was curled up asleep, so small that he looked like a black rock, a piece of coal, only soft, warm and breathing. I named him Joey after the song "Old Black Joe," because Joe, our Richmond yard man, had been nicer to me than anybody.

"Mein Gott! Un hund," Emmy said when she saw Joey.

"We'll keep him in the cage in the kitchen, Emmy. That way he'll be warm." Mommy smiled, as if she were handing out a prize. She nodded to Herr Prusnat who handed Emmy the cage.

"Yah, Frau Baldy." Emmy's smile reminded me of an animal baring its teeth.

I sat on the kitchen floor with Joey in my lap and listened to him breathe, feeling his tiny chest go up and down. Then I felt a warm smothering and then a hand shaking me.

"Wake up, Poodle." (Emmy had taken to calling me Poodle because of my curly hair.) "You've fallen into the rat's fur. Go to bed. Snell, snell!"

"I'm going, I'm going." Bleary-eyed, I tottered out of the kitchen up the stairs to bed, too sleepy to undress or even to clutch Raggedy Anne. But then I didn't need to clutch her. Finally, I had something live to hold.

When I got up the next morning, Emmy had already fed and watered Joey. "Ah, Poodle, speilen with your dog. I have enough vork than tend another baby—useless hund."

"He's not useless. He's my pet. I love him."

"What he do, except make pee-pee, poop, eat?" But she had already put rags in Joey's cage to make him more comfortable. "Animals, like people, should work." She strode to a cabinet and took out some flour and sugar. If she was going to bake, I didn't want to interrupt her.

"Hey, Joey; come Joey," I called. Joey didn't stir. "Joey!" I reached in the case and took him out. "Yikes, what's *that?* I screeched, as Joey let loose with a dribble. "Oooo," I said as Joey's pee trickled down the front of my blouse. In all my daydreams of having a dog, I'd never once thought of pee, poop or vomit. "Ugh, nasty!" I held Joey out in front of me, ran towards Emmy and thrust him at her.

"Ah, Poodle!" She wrapped Joey in a dishtowel.

Later, I remembered Mommy had said, "Daddy held you once. Then you wet on him. And he handed you back to me. He's not held you since." She usually laughed.

I knew that despite Mommy's saying I would have to take care of Joey, she had dumped Joey's care onto Emmy, and that I had done the same thing Daddy had by thrusting Joey at Emmy. It was weird. I had wet on Daddy and he had turned me over to Mommy forever. Joey had wet on me, and I had handed him to Emmy, the same thing.

Joey proved a huge disappointment, not like Cecil at all. Not only did he pee and throw up, but he couldn't do much of anything. Although Joey's eyes were open, they were so bleary, so he couldn't find his way around. All he wanted to do was snuggle into me or his blanket and sleep, eat, or lap water.

"This dog can't do anything! He can't fetch, jump, or even come when I call him," I said to Emmy.

"Naturally, Der hund is a kinder, like you, Poodle. Joey needs lessons. You teach him name, tricks, and trainings."

"I don't pee or spit up on myself! And I come when called, and I can fetch."

"Yah? And now know everything? You do all?"

Her sharp questions punctured me. "No, I can't do much of anything, change things. I want to, though."

"Want to learn, Poodle?" Emmy got out a big salt shaker.

"I guess so."

"Du learn when someone teaches—hund also."

So I decided to teach Joey to go up stairs even if it took a year. Anything would be better than being stuck with a boring dog. But when I set him on a bottom step, he just curled up against the rise.

"No, Joey. No. Climb." I picked him up and tried to steady him on all fours, but when I took my hand away, he collapsed and curled up again. "No, Joey!" I put a paw on the step and waited. Nothing happened, so I got up on the second step and coaxed.

"Come on, Joey. Come on?" Joey blinked. "Joey, come." I reached down and lifted a back log onto the stair. He stumbled and I barely caught him before he fell. A back leg was not the one to pick up. That close call scared me; lessons had to be over for that day. When I put Joey back in his cage, he crumpled into sleep.

"What's wrong with him? He sleeps all the time."

"Children, Poodle, sleep, Joey must sleep." Since Emmy took away the nasty part of taking care of him and Joey still snuggled, I decided to try the next day.

The next day I sat on the step above him and helped him up, and then began not to help so much, but coax him with words.

Finally, he climbed up on a stair, and I felt proud. All that day I carried him around, even wiping up pee spots from the floor

After that first victory, Joey learned to climb two steps more quickly than he did the first step, although he also tumbled a few times. I had to get watchful, so as catch him if he were about to tumble, for he would often twist in a really weird way and then fall. But I still caught him, every time. Once he caught on how to do it, he managed several steps at once. He just wanted to get where I was. I realized Joey couldn't help not being Cecil, although he was black like Cecil, and, like Cecil, he liked me. Joey was a baby. Besides, Cecil was a baby once, and even when grown up, still pooped inside and made Tom furious.

Finally, when Joey climbed the entire stairs to where I stood on the top landing. "Good, great!" I yelled, and Emmy came running.

"What?"

"Joey did it, climbed up—all the way to the top! Let's have a party!"

"Bah." She strode back to the kitchen.

In just a short time, Joey was scampering up the stairs and curling up on the bed with me. Like Cecil, he followed me everywhere. After a time, he began barking and pouncing on things like dust bunnies or on nothing at all. This jumping made Mommy and Daddy jumpy and cross. They were convinced Joey was pouncy because he was a Water Spaniel, another name for Springer Spaniels. I put Joey in some water in the bathtub to see what would happen, but he just shivered and looked miserable. I thought he jumped because of roaches in the kitchen, but I didn't say so.

I found the roaches because one night I sneaked down to the kitchen to filch a cookie. Switching on the light, I saw billions of cockroaches scampering over the floor, counters, and cabinets. Joey was awake and just looking around.

"Help, help!" I yelled but nobody came. I flew back upstairs and hid under the covers. I waited a long time before I poked my head out to see if the evil things had followed me. They hadn't. I told Mommy but she didn't see any in the daytime. She did find dirty frying pans and got upset. "What filth! It's a wonder we're not all deathly sick!" She told Emmy she must wash them, no matter what, but Emmy never did. Emmy told me that washing would "unseason" them.

Joey got so big that when he ran around the house, he broke a couple of lamps and some Hummel figures, which I never liked anyhow. But Mommy got very mad and wanted to throw Joey out. Daddy said a hunting dog ought to be outside; then Joey could run off some "steam." I took him on some walks outside, but not long enough because it was so cold. As soon as it got a little warmer, Herr Prusnat showed up to ready the ground for planting. When he was there, I let Joey out without me. I knew if Joey got too cold or into trouble, Herr Prusnat would rescue him. Herr Prusnat was not so big that Joey couldn't reach him when he wanted to jump and put his paws on him, nor was he so small that when he jumped he could be knocked over.

Then I began leaving him with Herr Prusnat more and more, especially as he planted flowers along the driveway. I thought Joey would get interested in what was going on and he seemed to. Also, Herr Prusnat had picked up a little English and I wanted to know what it was like to be a Nazi. When I asked Herr Prusnat about the war, he just shook his head and said, "Das kleinest mann, das kleinest mann, he gets troubles." It took me a while to figure out that "das kleinest mann" was not a short man but someone without money.

***

Being outside seemed to solve the Joey problem until he started to snarl and growl. He would snap at people, particularly strangers. At first we just stepped out of the way and wondered why he was in a bad mood. Most of the time, he just snarled at a driver or a passerby, but one time, he jumped at the French ambassador's wife, when they came to dinner.

"Mon Dieu, un savage. Au secours!" She yelped and shrank back, spilling her wine on her blue satin dress. "Ah, quelle shock!"

she slumped into a chair and put her hand to her forehead as if she were going to faint.

"Oh, Margaux, let me help you. Here is a damp cloth." Mommy produced a lace handkerchief with which Mme. Duchamp covered her face. "I've never believed in having animals in the house."

"I'm getting him out! Come on, Joey, come on." I grabbed Joey by the collar and began dragging him out. Pulled him into the kitchen.

"Bloody Hell. Let's all have a drink and forget this ridiculous mutt," Daddy said. He started mixing martinis.

"Frank, you must consider sending your dog to obedience school." M. Duchamp sounded like a policeman scolding a drunk at an accident. He held out his arm for Mme. Duchamp to lean upon, which, from her chair, she did and pulled herself up.

I don't know how the dinner went but guess that it didn't go well. At cocktails, Mme. Duchamp didn't even pretend to socialize; she just crossed her legs and sulked. She seemed to revel in upsetting Mommy. She reminded me of Dawn.

To me, it was a lot of fuss over nothing. All that uproar because Joey jumped at her. He did show his teeth though, so maybe that's why. My parents seemed to think so too although they were worried about how to pay for her ruined dress; it was from Paris and expensive. Except for that, they almost thought it was funny.

"The dog has a sixth sense," Daddy smiled. "Joey knew she was really a snake, not a woman."

"Oh, Frank." Mommy giggled.

"We can't risk Joey's biting at strangers. What if he had attacked Hiram Goode?" Hiram Goode was Daddy's boss. "What if he had attacked General Eisenhower? We should sick Joey on Stalin, that bastard. What do you say we donate him to the CIA?" He held out his empty highball glass.

Mommy got a bottle off the tea table and refilled his glass. "Frank, he wouldn't. Joey knows Hiram. And Eisenhower? Stalin? You're getting carried away. Mme. Duchamp was a stranger.

Maybe he didn't like her smell. After all, it's spring, and he's sensitive, ready to mate."

"Mate? Ha-ha. Spring, huh?" He rolled his eyes at Mommy. I went to bed.

Nothing happened after that, except that Joey broke two gilded porcelain cups Mommy left out on the coffee table. Joey still snarled at strangers and jumped at them for no reason. None of us could figure it out; he had been such a friendly puppy.

One morning the light woke me up really early. I heard Hannahlore and Albert, the coke deliverer, laughing, so I went downstairs.

The kitchen door was partly open, and Joey was jumping at a piece of meat that Albert was dangling. Just as Joey thought he would get it, Albert snatched it away. At almost the same time, Hannahlore banged him on the nose with Queen Louise, an old broken Madame Alexander doll that I wouldn't let Mommy pitch. When she hit Joey, he whimpered. And someone, Albert, Hannahlore or Emmy would shout something in German like "Shoen!" Then it started again: Dangle meat; Joey jump. Sometimes Joey got meat; sometimes he didn't; sometimes he'd get hit, sometimes he wouldn't. But always one of them would yell something in German. Then I caught on that when Joey growled, he got the meat. Sometimes Hannahlore stuffed Queen Louise with a tidbit stuck in the missing half of her porcelain head, and Joey would snarl. Finally, he would attack the doll or Hannahlore. I was confused and couldn't stand to hear Joey whimper.

"What are you doing?" I popped out of hiding. Albert lowered the tidbit. His creased face smiled and he said something in German. Hannahlore put the doll on the counter and looked down, almost smiling, like a kid caught but not sorry.

"We are teasing," Emmy said. "Joey—getting big. Earn keep."

"What's keep?" Emmy laughed and gave me a tidbit, not meat but a cookie.

"Protect house, get thief. Go back to bed, Poodle. Too early for you."

I ate the cookie, but didn't go back to bed. All day I thought about what I saw. I didn't know exactly what they were doing, only that their teasing was making Joey growl. But I didn't tell anyone, just like I didn't tell about Manfried. It would have just gotten everyone in trouble, so should be classified.

A couple weeks later. I ran to pick up Joey to take him outside. I must have scared him, because he jumped, growled, and bit me on the forearm.

"Ow, Joey! What are you doing? No, Joey. No!"

He growled some more, but backed off and curled up. I looked at my arm and saw bite marks but no blood. Joey looked ashamed, like Cecil looked that first day when I petted him. I reached out to pet Joey. He crouched down, as if he expected me to hit him. I petted him, but didn't try to take him outside. I was mad and also disturbed. What if he broke the skin the next time? Since I knew what was probably still going on in the kitchen, Joey would probably get worse. So I told myself Mommy ought to know about the bite, but not about the kitchen teasing. At Villa Hugel, this would be termed Information Management.

When Mommy got home, I showed her the bite marks. "Hmm. Hmm." She turned my arm over and over. "What do you think made him bite?"

"I don't know."

If I told or even started to tell about the kitchen, I might tell that Manfred lived upstairs or that I knew refreshments were really whiskies and that Santa Claus wasn't real. It was all bottled up and telling might uncork the bottle and all that stuff would fizz over. I'd already betrayed Dawn's secret, and now Joey's in a way.

"Hmm. I think you'll be okay." Mommy said.

I went upstairs into a closet and cried.

Later, Mommy and Daddy didn't talk much to me about the bite. I could tell they were concerned by their scrutiny and their "How are you?" Mommy continued planning parties, and sometimes calling in for Daddy when he was "not feeling well," saying he couldn't come in for work. Daddy grew more absorbed with Villa Hugel stuff, the latest being something called "The ECA

Mission." For a few days, I was careful approaching Joey; but for the most part, things went on as usual, except that Joey played outside more.

***

The air was moist, like after a rain, but there had been no rain, a signal Spring would stay. The daffodils had come and gone, and I had just come in from gathering the few that were left, when Mommy called.

"Honey, can you come here for a minute?" She was in the living room counting how many people the furniture could sit for a party.

"You know, Honey, eventually we will move."

"Move?"

"I mean go home, back to the USA."

"Oh, yeah."

Then she went into a long thing about how, of course, we couldn't take Joey home and that perhaps we should let Herr Prusnat have him, since they were such good friends and since Joey would have plenty of time outdoors.

"How can Joey always have time outdoors, since Herr Prusnat won't be our gardener anymore when we leave?"

"I'm sure Herr Prusnat has a big yard with a garden; he loves plants so. Besides, he may get another gardening job, because what else can he do now? Germany is still a mess; the Marshall Plan will take years to finish."

"Oh." I swallowed that Herr Prusnat would have a large yard, which he probably didn't.

"How would you feel if Joey went to live with Herr Prusnat?"

"When we move?"

"No, Honey, now."

"Oh." My stomach dropped. I knew the "now" was because of my bite. I'd never told on the servants teasing Joey. Now I wanted to get even if they did get in trouble. So I told about the kitchen help being mean and hitting Joey.

"Well, that is unfortunate," Mommy said after I told her. "But it doesn't change things does it?" I didn't answer. "Do you want to think about it?"

I nodded and went upstairs to my room. Once there I didn't grab Raggedy Ann and pulled at only a couple of cuticles. Instead I looked out the front window. Outside were large patches of green grass, and small buds on trees. Beyond our yard were other big houses with big yards and trees. Beyond them small houses, like Irmgard's place and the rubble-studded center of Heisingen; somewhere beyond brooded, massive Villa Hugel. I was sure Villa Hugel had caused all this trouble, although no one said so.

I knew my parents wanted to get rid of Joey to protect me from more bites. But how could they just turn him out like he was nobody? And how could Emmy and Albert who were so nice to me, make Joey so mean? I knew they had made him bite and were probably still doing that. Even if Mommy and Daddy told them to stop, would they? The frying pans remained unwashed. Come to think of it, I'd never seen a big dog that wasn't a guard dog or an attack dog. The little dogs, especially the long-haired wiener pooches, were the ones that stayed inside. Emmy, Hannahlore and Albert hadn't flinched when Joey whimpered and had praised him when he growled. Germans weren't monsters like GIs said; I knew that much now. Then why were they acting like ones?

The rumbling noise of a Mercedes startled me. It drove up to our iron gate, and the driver got out and opened it wide. Daddy was coming home from Villa Hugel. Soon the evening routine would begin: Emmy's asking Mommy about dinner; Mommy's preparing the first drink, Daddy's changing into his velvet smoking jacket. The endless talk would begin and continue into dinner and afterwards.

To me, Villa Hugel, dinner, Daddy's rants, my parents' good intentions, even my bite didn't matter. Only Joey mattered. Joey might be almost grown but was still young. He should be romping and making messes inside or out. If I said no to Herr Prusnat, would what happened to Donald happen to Joey? I didn't want to think about it. I wanted Joey to be happy, happy for a long time, and he would be if he lived with Herr Prusnat. So I had to tell Mommy yes; that was the best way, maybe the only way, even if it was hard. This time I wasn't powerless; this time I could do something; I could let Joey go.

I wiped the blood off my cuticles, so no one would notice. As I went down the stairs to tell Mommy, something else ripped in me, like when Granddaddy died.

Chapter Four

Christmas and Choking on Sauerbraten

Joey, my spaniel, was gone. Mommy and Daddy were gone. Even Irmgard was visiting some cousin. Villa Hugel's swimming pool was closed because it was cold. It rained or snowed all the time and got dark early. You couldn't see the village clock because of fog, only hear it sometimes. Even without the clock, I knew when it was four because then Emmy would lower the wooden blinds, clackity, clack. Four O'clock.

If I read *Little Women* over, I'd throw up, and I was also tired of *Reader's Digest*. There was nothing else to read except *Stars and Stripes* "New Year 1950" issue.

So I went outside and stuck my tongue out to catch the flakes, but the wind stung my eyes. So I came in but couldn't find anybody. Then I went upstairs. Emmy was rearranging stuff in the hall linen closet.

"Emmy, I'm hungry. I want some sauerbraten."

Emmy turned her head; a few hairs stuck out from her hair bun. "Nein. Dinner is at nine; you will wait." She gave me a half-smile, and went back to stacking. That made me mad.

"The sauerbraten is left-over. Daddy doesn't like leftovers, so you won't give us that for dinner."

"Dinner ready at nine o'clock." She was stacking nice napkins in one pile, everyday ones in another, and raggedy ones in another. One hand would grab a napkin, pass it to the other and both would fold, 1, 2, 3. Quick.

"Why are you stacking rags? That's a waste of time." Emmy grabbed another rag. "Stop that. I'm hungry!"

"You had cocoa and cookies an hour ago." She was stacking really high. I hoped they would fall. "And you have cocoa on your dress, the top part. Take one of these, wet it and wash off the cocoa before it stains."

"I'm hungry!" I stamped my foot. "Fix me something to eat."

She stopped. "You are not to shout at me, ever!" Her eyes were yellow, like a cat's.

I began to fake cry. "You don't care about me; you would let me starve. I hate you! You never do anything for me. I have nothing to do, am hungry, and you can't think of anything but your stupid linens."

"They are your mother's linens. You will not eat. You will not yell at me ever." Emmy peered down her hook nose, hands on her hips, elbows out. "Is this *clear?*" She glared at me—a witch. I ran and knocked the stacks onto the floor. "Maria!" She yelled as I knocked the stacks as I ran down the stairs.

I hid in a closet under the stairs, but heard nothing, only smelled cabbage cooking. Finally, I went into the winter garden and saw plants with bugs. So I went to the laundry room where Hannahlore hid soap scraps behind clothespins. I poured some scraps into a spray bottle of water, then went back and sprayed aphids. I'd read that spraying aphids would kill them, and I wanted to kill something. Spray, spray—kill, kill—but as I picked off aphids, I realized Emmy could keep me safe, even if she was mean—or maybe because she was mean. She'd kicked a man in the market who tried to lift food out of her basket, and she'd yelled at Dawn, even Dawn, when she caught Dawn eying coins on a coffee table. In the war, did she dress like a Nazi officer, so nobody would know she was a girl? Yet still Emmy'd cared for me when I vomited. She protected Manfried, and didn't tell on me when I got sick at Christmas from eating too many springerle cookies. She could rescue me from a fire, could fight burglars. She would do it, even if I was bad. Emmy did not have migraines or heart attacks like Mommy.

When the bottle was empty, there was hardly any light in the winter garden, and the blinds had already clacked down. I was tiptoeing through the dining room when I saw beside my chair a plate of sauerbraten. Emmy had heated it up, after all.

I grabbed the fork and jammed sauerbraten into my mouth. It was cold and slimy, like cooked okra or a bugger. It didn't even have that "once good" flavor. The meat must have set out a long time. I felt sad, kind of like missing a party, but more like finding out about the tooth fairy. Before, I could boss Irmgard, but never Emmy. She was stronger than anyone, even Americans. Now I knew she wasn't really. She had to heat up the food, especially since Mommy was coming back. Even if Emmy had been a super-Nazi during the war, now she was the maid—only the maid. She had to do what I said to keep herself, not me, safe. Then the food choked me, and I began to cry.

***

Unlike other children, I was not particularly fond of Christmas, although I pretended to be and occasionally convinced myself. To me Christmas meant a lot of presents for me with parents looking on but not really saying much. Daddy would concentrate on Christmas cheer and Mommy would disappear into the kitchen to cook. Daddy would pass out before dinner was ready, and Mommy would be sad. There was never anyone to play with. That was what happened in Richmond. In Atlanta, when Daddy didn't have a job, we shared a house with another family, where the adults would do just about the same thing. But there were other people there, teen-agers, who ate with me. So Christmas in Atlanta wasn't bad, just not great. So I expected Christmas in Essen would be more like it was in Richmond because we didn't share a house.

Our tree was in the circular "den"—a tanenbaum. The night before, red-cheeked children with multicolored mittens and wool hats that came all the way over their ears, serenaded us. Carols, I suppose. Those hats and gloves looked like grandmothers had knitted them, and that made me jealous. German children had to be different. For one thing, they had to be healthier; their cheeks were so red and their voices so clear. No sinus problems or Kleenex anywhere. But of course, with grandmothers, they wouldn't have those problems.

But in the following Christmas seasons the best part of the long days between the Lantern Parade, St. Nicholas Day and Christmas became watching Emmy, the housekeeper, bake

Christmas cookies. That was almost as good as having a grandmother. Emmy's baking involved blizzards of flour, diamond grains of sugar and full, pale moons of butter. She would stand rocket straight in a faded green bib apron and wield a wood rolling pin big as a roll of toilet paper. "Squish, squish" went the sugar, flour, and butter as they glopped beneath the rolling pin. "Slap, slap" sounded the dough as she air lifted it, and then slapped down over and over on the floury counter. Then she turned the great pin on its end, on one of its pencil-thick handles, pounded, pounded the dough.

Near the sink were wood rectangles with cut-out figures of St. Nicholas, angels, stars. Their bottoms were rough; no one took the time to smooth them. All kitchen surfaces got frosted with flour, and the wood crackled so loud in the stove that sometimes I'd say, "Isn't it time to put those in the oven? Aren't you hot, Emmy?" Emmy then would glance at me with a hawk's eye; her hook nose a beak to pierce me. She'd swoop sheets of dough over the wood cutouts, press dough into them, knife off excess and then slide them into the oven. When the wood slabs come out, the Springerles are toast at the edges and moon pale on the rest. The cookies will stick because of the roughness inside. Emmy tapped the wood against the porcelain sink, and then St. Nicks, angels, trees and stars dropped onto the floured cloth—another piece of magic.

On Christmas morning I got a set of pottery. On each plate, cup and saucer were little elves with turned-up noses, pointy hats, wild flowers and big red mushrooms with white polka dots. These were elves that lived in the woods, magic elves. I also got clothes, books, and a German picture book called *Struwwelpeter*. After the unwrapping everything, the room was covered in ribbons and paper. I moved and crunched some paper, then saw beneath a giant piece of crumpled wrapping paper a tiny wrapped present! I tore off the paper in about 15 seconds, lifted the lid off of the small box, saw a layer of cotton wool. Underneath that cotton lay a watch. The watch had a copper-colored frame and easy to read numbers on its face. The watchband was of a dark red suede material.

I had forgotten all about my Christmas wish to the landlady. She hadn't. The memory of her shocked face reoccurs to me now, almost sixty years later. What I didn't know then was that any kind of timepiece during that period cost a small fortune. The house's owner, whom the allies had forced to live in her own basement, had somehow managed to provide not only a Gingerbread House, but a watch.

I was very excited. So was Mommy. "How sweet!" she said.

But Daddy, already on his second bourbon and water, was scowling. "We can't let her accept this. It's inappropriate." He swished his ice cubes. They made an ominous tinkle. "No telling how it would be read."

"No, no!" I clutched my wrist, for by then I had it on.

"Now, Frank," Mother soothed. The wrangle began and I burst into tears, a typical Christmas. I ran upstairs to my room and wiped my tears on Raggedy Ann. Downstairs, I heard the indignation turning into a rant, and Mother's saying, "Yes, dear, or yes, but." After a while, I went downstairs to play with my new china and to be near them, even though they were still quietly fighting. I told myself if I couldn't keep the watch, I had other presents, and so what was the big deal? This was just another typical Christmas, something to be endured.

But it *wasn't* typical; First of all, it was Germany and Mother had no Christmas dinner to fix as we were going out. Instead, she poured another and then another for Daddy, all the time patiently holding her ground and listening to him rant. The rant mellowed into a kind of refrain, a garbled refrain. Over and over, Daddy asked, "So, you think it's all right? You think it would be all right?" and watched Mother nod. Since coming to Germany, he was always worried about something, probably money. Anyway, I was used to it. Worry was just another adult quirk. I couldn't know that he worried that the watch might be construed as a bribe or about an impending Russian invasion from East Germany.

"It's all right," she'd interject. Then began the questioning all over again. Mother would pick up her knitting; between stitches she'd chant "Yes, it will be all right. It will be fine."

The tea table's liquor bottles, sodas and ice bucket slowly emptied, but at faster rate than when we first moved into the house. When late afternoon came and they had to dress for wherever they were going, Daddy was wobbly, but not passed out. I never had to take off the watch. And didn't, not even sixty years later.

Chapter Five

Irmgard, Villa Hugel, and a Brat

There was no American school in the area, so I had nothing to do but read more Nancy Drew mysteries. I always came back to her. She offered unpredictability, unlike other "children's books." First, there were no "happily ever afters"—she simply solved one mystery, not a whole life; second, no one had to tell her anything. She snooped on her own, and, unlike grown-ups, put together pieces of information in unconventional, surprising ways. Also, she invented pithy phrases, like in *The Scarlet Slipper Mystery*: "Always remember, writers of anonymous notes are cowards."

Like I said before, my favorite pastime was swimming in Villa Hugel's indoor pool. Emmy would take me and wait while I swam. To get to Villa Hugel someone had to phone a "car pool" to get a Mercedes. I assumed that because these black cars had names, that they were special cars reserved for taking people to pools.

But reading and swimming by myself was lonely, so I began walking to market with Emmy. When she took her fishnet-like sling bag off the hook, I raced to get my coat. The walk was long and cold, but worth it to see the bustling shoppers arguing about prices and pinching cabbages. One day at this market I met Irmgard who, like Emmy, was examining the onions.

Irmgard was fourteen, almost five years older than I. She had frizzy dark blonde hair; small humps perked the bodice of her dress. Even more impressive than her budding womanliness was her halting English.

"Is you here to get food for family?" she asked. I grinned and shook my head and looked at the floor. But the friendship had already begun. Irmgard began to come to my house and listen to my tales of the states. Finally, she took me to her house.

Although it was afternoon, Irmgard's tiny house was dark inside, except for wood burning in the iron stove. Irmgard's father's face, creased like folded paper, seemed preserved in contemplation. He was smoking a pipe and in all my visits, I never saw him put down his pipe or stir from the kitchen table. Near him, on a high hook, hung a stained military uniform. Irmgard's mother stood ironing near the stove, sweat misting her forehead and half-moons darkening her underarm sleeves. She had five irons of graduated sizes on the stove. One would heat on a burner; she would grab it, put another on the burner, and iron with the first one. When the one she was using cooled, she picked up the one that was warming, until that one cooled. I had only seen an electric iron, never anything as fancy as this. I didn't know Irmgard had a brother, so was surprised to meet twenty-year-old Franz, back from somewhere. Franz was tall with dark, longish hair. His pallid face already had creases like his father's. He looked like Prince Valiant, my comic book hero. When he clicked his heels and kissed my hand, I fell instantly in love.

Perhaps I was aping other diplomatic brats, but after a while I began to throw my weight around with Irmgard. Starting with Sondra's party, I'd seen that children of official Americans, British or French, ordered servants around and were often rude to anyone, but usually to Germans. A French kid, I barely knew, yelled when the maid wanted to draw the curtains. Dawn sent food back that the cook had made especially for her. "Are you stupid?" she cried. She stamped her foot. "You know I don't like toast 'light.'" Once, I tried ordering Emmy around, but it didn't work. Irmgard, however, was a different matter. I could demand she come to my house or order her to go home, according to my whim. And she would obey. Despite this, or perhaps because of Irmgard's placid disposition, we stayed friends.

One cold, rainy afternoon, Irmgard and I had played checkers and read *Struwwelpeter*. Now I was bored and wanted to go swimming. Despite the coal shortage, the pool would be heated; Villa Hugel always had heat. "Irmgard, would you like to go swimming?"

"Swimming? All closed in winter."

"No swimming!" Emmy yelled from the kitchen, wringing a mop so hard, the veins in her forearms stood out. She was on a cleaning rampage and had two buckets and various mops, brooms and rags in each room of the house. The more she cleaned, the more worked up she got. "No swimming! Must work."

"Please, please. If Irmgard goes, you wouldn't have to go; she can instruct the driver. All you'd have to do is call the car pool."

Irmgard turned to me. "I'll have to ask my parents."

"Why? You don't ask permission to come here."

"It's different." Irmgard took off on her bicycle.

It was a ten-minute bike ride to Irmgard's house, but she didn't return for an hour. Then she had changed in a fresh-faded dress and a sweater.

On the way to Villa Hugel, the driver and Irmgard talked but her voice was shrill and she sat too straight. As we drove up to the sooty mansion, Irmgard shrank back in the seat. I jumped out and headed for the entrance and had already grasped the door handle when I realized I didn't hear Irmgard's step. I turned and saw her huddled against the Mercedes. "Come on!" I waved her in. "Come on, so the car can go!"

Irmgard shuffled up to the portico. Shivering, she wrapped her arms around herself; "No."

"What do you mean no?" I pointed to the bundle she carried. "You brought your suit. She clasped her package more tightly. Although it was drizzling and I had no umbrella, I went to her. "What's wrong, Irmgard?"

"I can't, I can't." Irmgard's chin trembled, and she gurgled.

"Why can't you? Why?"

Her shoulders heaved. "It's mighty—too mighty for me."

"Oh, don't be stupid. It's for Americans and British now."

But she kept snuffling. All I could get out of her was that her family didn't "go with Krupps."

"Why, why not?"

Irmgard said that families like hers didn't go to rich people's houses. It just wasn't done. Her grandmother, or great grandmother, had shown up at Villa Hugel to do laundry, but the guards wouldn't let her in. When she tried to tell them she had a duty there, they beat her up. Bad things would happen if a "low" family came to Villa Hugel.

"Besides your grandmother or whoever, what kind of bad things?" I tried to talk sense into her. "After all, she's dead."

"Father told me people go in there and never come back." Her shoulders drooped.

"People? What kind of people?"

"Lots, many, many, some who couldn't speak German." Irmgard sighed. "They came from there." She swung her arm towards the East. "For work and war."

Villa Hugel was mammoth. Krupp would need lots of people to clean and maintain it. So what if the maids didn't speak German, as long as they cleaned well?

Then, Irmgard's war excuse didn't make sense. I didn't know about forced labor, even what the term meant, much less that 140,000 people from the East, mainly Poland, had been kidnapped and made slaves in Krupp's industries, forced to make armaments for World War II. Sixty years later, when I looked at the Krupp-Hitler letter in Villa Hugel museum, I realized Irmgard was not lying, and I want to find her and apologize. But to me then, Irmgard was simply lost in the family past and old war scare stories. Then, to me, truth was obvious: people came out of Villa Hugel as well as went in, like we did. Besides, if so many went in, eventually even Villa Hugel would get crowded, and people would have to leave. No. Irmgard was just superstitious; she might as well have been talking about trolls.

"Look, the war's over and your grandmother's dead. You brought your suit and got your parents' permission, *permission!* We're so close to the pool. Let's just go!" I walked through the doors and waved at her. Because of the cold, she finally came just inside but wouldn't go further. When I pulled on her elbow, she jerked it back. "What is the matter with you? Are you crazy?" I grabbed her arm again.

Then out of the blue, she said loudly, "You love my brother!"

"What?" How had she guessed? I felt myself go red in the face. "No, no, I don't. I don't even know your brother."

Irmgard turned to one of the British guards. "She loves him; she doesn't want to be found out."

"Irmgard!" I stamped my foot. Irmgard smoothed her apron, her square jaw set like concrete. "Yes, you love him and he knows it. He laughs at you!"

"Shut up!"

Then the British guard winked. He winked! I thought I would die. After that wink, I would do anything to shut Irmgard up. "Okay, okay, Irmgard....but why?"

"Krupp up, up high." She raised her hand above her head. "I should not go in there."

"You are such a twit! I told you—Americans and English own this now? We are democratic—everyone's equal. Are you stupid or what?" Some staff members turned and looked at us, but Irmgard did not budge. "What do you want?" I pushed her.

"Home." Irmgard looked up for the first time her eyes were hooded. "Or I tell all people you love Franz."

We walked back to the car pool and found the driver, and he brought us home.

***

Later, I became determined to get her into that pool. First I taunted her: "Yah, yah—Kraut, Kraut, Sauerkraut—scared of a little American girl."

Then I'd be nice. I brushed her hair and got the frizz out, sneaked her peanut butter from the commissary, and even gave her Mother's lipstick from the PX lipstick, thinking Mommy wouldn't miss it—she didn't.

Also I'd try to make her feel guilty. "Why won't you go, Irmgard, after all I've done for you?" I'd tell her that because she was my only friend, she *had* to go. "Besides, how can you people learn that we are equal, don't you get it? It's a new world now. No class stuff, at least among Americans.

Finally, she agreed. But when we did, it wasn't fun. Once past the entrance, Irmgard cowered near a suit of armor.

"Still scared?" I asked.

She nodded.

"Look, Irmgard, everything is all bright. The chandeliers are lit. There are no dark corners, so absolutely *no* reason for you to be afraid. I pushed her towards the small door that led to the basement and the pool. Come on."

As we rocketed through the immense kitchens, Irmgard gawked at the huge pots, pans and knives.

When Irmgard saw the beautiful green-and-white-tiled swimming room, she stood stock still, looking as if she were going to cry again.

"Too beautiful," she said and began snuffling again.

"Come on." I jostled her arm. "Let's change."

In the pool, we thrashed about competing for the biggest water smack, but never managed more than mild splashes. As we swam, the pool's chlorine smell blended with the rotten smell of mold and bothered Irmgard. As long as it didn't reach the pool, I didn't care. After our swim we went into the Kaiser's shower, but the shower head was still rusted. Only giant tears dripped onto us and the tiny checked, white-tiled floor, blop, blop, clop, clop.

When we were finished and waiting to be picked up, I wanted to point out how silly her fears had been.

"There, see—it wasn't so bad, was it?" I said.

Just then a Mercedes pulled up for us. Irmgard just shook her head and got in the car.

We went swimming twice more at Villa Hugel pool. Then Irmgard quit going. She claimed the mold bothered her, or that her mother wouldn't let her go. But she was lying. Each time we walked through the Great Room to the basement stairs, she kept her head down and thought people were staring at her.

My last Christmas in Essen, Irmgard gave me a handkerchief she'd embroidered herself. I gave her a Brownie box camera. We sat in front of the fireplace, arms around each other. Again I asked why she had been scared at Villa Hugel.

"I will be punished for being there," she sighed, "but don't know when." Then she didn't realize that through me, she'd been punished not only for making her swim in a place she didn't like, but for telling me the truth about Villa Hugel's past. Despite my cant of equality, I'd used my superior position of conqueror to bully her, just as I'd seen other diplomatic brats wield power to get their way.

Chapter Six

Dr. Kort's Sabers

When Dr. Kort first came to us I wondered why the Allies hadn't sent an American or British doctor. Nonetheless, Dr. Kort's super-tall, super-large frame with a laugh to match made him an imposing man. Also, he fit into our large Elasse Strasse house, like a chinois shrunk that was always there but that we had failed to notice. Dr. Kort's ruddy face contrasted with his grey or black three-piece suit, its vest covering his round belly like a custom-made glove. Dr. Kort's belly wasn't a camel's hump or a pot turned upside down in a skinny body like Daddy's, but more of a natural hill, sloping gently up from his chest, peaking at his middle, then curving down to his groin,

My father looked the opposite of Dr. Kort. Daddy kept getting thinner, paler and wrinklier. He drank and drank and talked more about the red tapes, and the Reds. Worse, now he was sounding like the Sergeants: Korea, Korea, Korea. Like Krupp, this stupid country was also mixed up with red tapes and Reds. Was Daddy going to suddenly leave, like the Sergeants did? I didn't think so because he looked so pale; the sergeants looked a whole lot healthier. But it didn't really matter where Daddy was because he was hardly ever home anyway; only this time, I knew where he'd be—at Villa Hugel, doing coal stuff. Daddy was better than those Sergeants. He was honest and didn't lie. He had only one wife and one kid; although I think Mommy wanted more.

Dr. Kort doctored everybody at Villa Hugel, and although nobody at our house was sick, he came regularly to give Daddy shots, which was odd. Daddy seemed to look forward to them or maybe to seeing Dr. Kort, because I can't imagine anyone liking shots.

I could tell when Dr. Kort was coming because Mommy would get excited.

"Oh, my, Frank, tomorrow? I don't know if we can get ready in time," she'd say but she always did. Then she'd instruct Emmy to prepare a splendid Second Breakfast, which I'd never heard of because we hardly had a first breakfast, at least together. Later, Emmy told me that Second Breakfast was a tradition, that one might have a coffee and roll early in the morning but later have a *real* breakfast, and that it was a fun thing.

"Yah, yah," Frau Baldy," Emmy would say when Mommy would order a Second Breakfast, "And will you want linens on the oval table?" Mommy would nod and then she and Emmy would decide on what to serve and how to do it. I kept waiting for the fun part.

Daddy's shots must have been given in his bottom, because when Dr. Kort came, he and Daddy always went to a room by themselves. When they came out, talking, if Joachim, Dr. Kort's son, was there to translate, Mommy would say. "Ah, Dr. Kort, it is late. Won't you join us for the Second Breakfast?"

"Ah, Nein, nein, Frau Baldy, I am too fat already." Dr. Kort would pat his stomach and laugh. His laugh was a deep "Ho, ho, ho," like Santa probably laughs, except Santa brings presents, not shots.

"Oh, please, Dr. Kort, honor us. You do us so much good," Mommy would say, wring her hands a little, as if begging, and he would always stay.

The best parts about Dr. Kort's visits were the baking smells before he came and eating the baked breads and rolls when he was here. The morning air would be filled with the aromas of croissants baking, braided raisin breads and roasting, sugar-glazed almonds. Emmy somehow got jars of homemade jam but wouldn't tell me where or how. The worst part about his visits was that I had to sit through the "Second Breakfast," which started about ten, right after Daddy's shot and lasted past noon. All that time, they ate and blah-blah-blahed. Mommy would sometimes try to translate, because she was taking German lessons ("the grammar is so hard"), but most of the time Dr. Kort's son Joachim translated. It was all really boring except one time I noticed something which explained a lot about Dr. Kort.

One Second Breakfast, I started staring at Dr. Kort's face when he was laughing at some joke he'd made. As he turned his face to avoid the mid-morning glare, I noticed that one wrinkle didn't look like the others. Why not? What was it? It was a scar, a long, curved scar, like Mommy's and on the same side too. A mystery. Why did he have a scar?

"Nancy Drew always listened more than she talked. Nancy Drew waited for "free information," so I decided to do the same. But when Dr. Kort wasn't at our house, nobody discussed him, so there wasn't any free information. So I decided to bring it up.

"Mommy, how did Dr. Kort get his scar?" I asked her one morning when she was making a list for "arranging things."

"What scar?"

"The scar on his left cheek, same as yours. That one."

"I haven't noticed any scar. Drat!" She broke her pencil point.

But Dr. Kort had made so many visits; how could she have not noticed that he had a scar?

"I don't know Mary Hanford. I'm just focused on what he's doing for your father." She started rifling through her purse. After she fished out a ball point pen, she tossed me her Run-Along-Now-Smile.

"Honey, I have to write invitations that must go out today. I don't have time to speculate about scars." Mommy sat on a spindly chair in front of her desk. The desk was called a Spinet desk and had also belonged to Aunt Natalie.

So I knew that it was time for me to shut up, watch, wait and learn. Nancy Drew always got quiet when she was onto something. I went to my room to reread some Nancy Drew mysteries to figure out how Nancy would handle this dilemma. It was just too weird, both of them having the same scars in the same places.

***

But I didn't find a solution in the books, so at the next Sunday breakfast, right after the first "brot" and jam, I spoke up.

"Where did you get that scar on your face, Dr. Kort?"

"Mary Hanford, for heaven's sake, that's a personal question." Mommy's eyes widened.

"Das kleinest machen—ha, ha. She is quiet but she observes." Dr. Kort looked proud, as if I'd won a prize. His look warmed me to my toes, like hot chocolate does.

"It's like Mommy's. Look." I pointed to the scar on her left cheek.

"Oh, Mary Hanford," Mommy fluttered.

"Aha! Vos es los?" Dr. Kort peered at her, and Mommy was stuck with explaining. .

"Ah, yah, yah," Dr. Kort nodded as she told her story.

"Ah, but my scar was deliberate, not like yours, Frau Baldy."

He turned towards me. "I got *my* scar at college. Unlike Mama's, it was no accident." He traced his forefinger from the top of the scar, near his eye all the way down its end, a little space away from his upper lip.

I wanted to say but didn't that Mommy's scar was not an accident either. She intended to shave, just like her daddy.

"Do you want to touch it, Machen, see if it is real?" Dr. Kort thrust out his cheek and I put my finger on it; it felt like rubber, not soft like regular skin. Also there was no hair-fuzz on the scar.

Dr. Kort explained that in college he had to get a scar, a saber scar. To join something he had to fight someone with a special sword, a saber. The scar was curved because it had been made by a saber which was curved. A saber scar was an honor that proved your mettle in college.

No wonder there had been a war.

Daddy had told me college was where people learned great ideas, particularly at Harvard. So college people should teach people to be peaceful, not to cut each other up. Something wasn't right.

Suddenly, like one of Nancy's flashes, I deduced the truth: Dr. Kort was a Nazi, or had been, an important one! The club he had to get hurt to join was the Nazi club. Kort was doctoring the Allies, so he wouldn't go to jail like the Krupp guy. Elementary, my dear

Nancy. After all, the Krupp man only made guns. Dr. Kort fought with knives which were worse than guns; because they hurt longer. Dr. Kort had to serve the Allies or be in *huge* trouble.

I looked at Daddy, who'd been slumped in his chair, while the scar talk was going on. Emmy came in for the third time bringing more coffee and new hot rolls, this time with poppy seeds on top. There was a little commotion over the rolls and about passing the butter, which made Daddy sit up and pay attention. Then he started in *again* about Korea.

"Who knows when this will end? The Communists are more focused, not scattered as our forces, half of which are here in Germany." Daddy took a bite of Emmy's roll. "It was a scandal how we got into this, as if we didn't have enough trouble. Mark my words, this can't have a definitive ending—we can't atom bomb Korea. How much blood...." He took another bite. "The USA will have to get manpower, materiel and leaders from somewhere...he finished the roll, then swiped a huge linen napkin across his mouth.

"Yah, yah." Dr. Kort had stopped joking. He didn't stop eating, though.

"May I be excused?" I asked.

Mommy nodded, and I went up to my room. There was no sense in listening to more Korea stuff. I'd heard it all before. Even so, I couldn't figure out what was really going on about Korea. No one else seemed to know either.

***

In my room, I thought and thought. Like Nancy, I had to consider the situation and its probable consequences. In this case, Dr. Kort's Nazi background plus his propensity for knives, made him a dangerous character. He wasn't as placid as Heinz at Ayre House, and even Heinz had gotten mad. Who knew when Daddy might say the wrong thing, and Dr. Kort might turn his needles into knives and kill him? What if he could somehow make knives look like big syringes, the kind that people give horses? The possibilities were legion. There was only one solution. I had to protect my father.

***

When Monday came, and Daddy had gone to Villa Hugel, I tip-toed into their huge bedroom before Mommy had "her face on." She was seated on a stool before a mirror brushing her light brown hair; the morning light was streaming through the windows and through her hair. I saw that she really didn't have much, as her scalp showed through in the light. And I worried that it would all come out, she brushed so hard.

"Mommy, you know Dr. Kort?" She nodded, and put a couple of bobby pins in her mouth.

"Why does he come so often? What are those shots for?" I suspected she didn't know.

"Vitamin B 12 shots; shots to build your father up." She took a bobby pin out of her mouth and pinned some hair back, behind her ear.

"Build him up for what? Isn't he already built up?" Out came the other bobby pin and hid in a place close to her neck. Her brown hair was curly as mine; but not so dark. Also, it never got frizzy, only limp looking because it was so thin.

"So he'll be strong and healthy and can do his job."

"Isn't he doing it now?"

"Of course, but if he felt stronger, he could handle Korea if he is sent there." She pinned up another hank of hair into a twist at the back, and then fluffed out the sides with a rat-tailed comb. Now she looked like she had more hair. "And he worries about us, what would happen to us if he went."

Korea. *That* word again. "Why is he worrying more? What would happen to us if he goes to Korea?"

"Nothing, probably. Oh, we might have to move out of this big house, but I doubt it."

"That's all?"

"Probably, if that."

"But he'd have no more shots from Dr. Kort, right?"

"Right. The time for that would be over," Mommy said.

Relief flooded me. "Whew." I wouldn't have to do anything to save him.

"Whew. What do you mean? Whew?" Mommy smiled softly, as if a small joke.

With her hair fancied up, Mommy looked like a china doll in her green velvet robe, maybe a fat doll, but a doll like our Royal Doulton dolls, "Rose" or "The Sheppardess." I'd been warned about that so many times that those porcelain dolls, if accidently knocked off a shelf, would smash. Mommy's feelings could be smashed. She'd shown that when the French snubbed her. Maybe I shouldn't tell her the truth about Dr. Kort. If Daddy was in Korea, he would be out of harm's way anyhow. Why risk upsetting her? She already had heart trouble.

"Oh, nothing, really. Just thinking about my massive assignment about …" I couldn't think of a subject, so gave a fake sigh.

"Better do it now then. You'll be relieved when it's finished," Mommy broke in and went to the long cedar closet to pick out something to wear.

"Yes, Mommy, I will."

The closet's delicious cedar smell swept over me, and suddenly I wanted to be outdoors. Since I was saved from saving anyone, I went to find Herr Prusnat and to see if he had brought Joey with him.

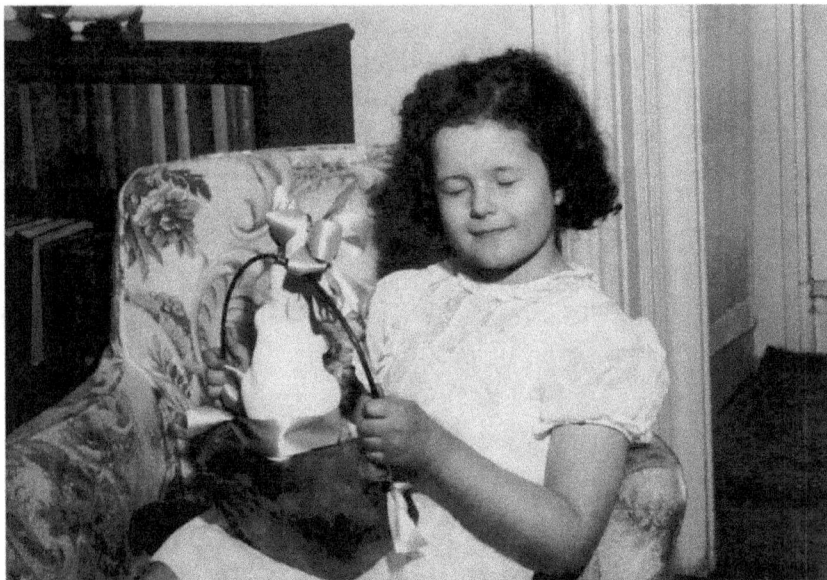

Atlanta, Georgia, 1949 or 1950
just before embarking for Germany

7 Elasse Strasse in Heisingen, a suburb of Essen where I lived for two years. Picture was taken in 1950.

*1952 School picture of American school in Bad Godesburg,
suburb of Bonn where I spent only a few months.*

The American School that was pictured earlier.

This was taken in 1950, right after I turned ten years old in Ayre House in Essen. The poodle is Cecil, who belonged to Tom Hitchman, a resident with a broken leg.

Atlanta, Georgia 1949

My father, mother and a German woman.
Picture was taken in 1951 or 1952 in Bad Godesburg,
just before going on a boat trip on the Rhine.

The address of our Bad Godesburg apartment building was 19 Europa Strasse. I took the picture in 1952.

Taken in Essen, Germany in 1950 at a boring birthday party for child front center. I had to go because it was the "diplomatic" thing to do.

Birthday party for Sondra, who turned three in Essen, Germany in 1950.

*Taken in 1951 or 1952 on a boat trip on the Rhine.
I am the curly-haired one in the striped shirt,
which was navy and white.*

Waiting room to a diplomatic office.

One of the roads to Villa Hugel.
It was there in 1950 and still stands.

I returned to Villa Hugel's pool in 2009, sixty years later. Nothing has changed except the pool is now dry and off limits to the public.

Chapter Seven

Calvert School Dropout

The Calvert Course was a correspondence course for diplomats' children who had no American school to attend. Designed around the American public school curriculum, it claimed that no child would be held back in American education because of living abroad. As in proper schools, the student had to complete the lessons in a timely manner in order to complete a grade. "Timely manner" didn't mean anything. There wasn't any real deadline and no teacher to prod or explain. Mommy had all the materials spread out on a special table in my room, but I didn't finish even two lessons.

Instead, I retreated into the welcoming palms and ferns of the winter garten. After Herr Prusnat treated them, the air felt like a beach and smelled like grass. The sun and/or snow made the place the brightest in the house, and there I delved into the latest Nancy Drew and Bobsey Twins mysteries. After a while, I saw through the Bobsey Twins plot formula, so took to checking the end first, hoping for unpredictability. There wasn't any, so I stuck with Nancy Drew. She was older than I, but not much and had a car, a convertible. Even my parents didn't have a car! The main draw was that Nancy was competent, Unlike Amy, or even Meg, in *Little Women,* whose main functions seemed to be charm and look pretty, Nancy did both. She could both look pretty and solve mysteries. Further, she always seemed to know what to do in any circumstance. For instance, I'd never thought that "Red Lipstick makes a great window SOS," [*Mystery of the Fire Dragon*] or that "A beret is the perfect accessory when you need to conceal a stash of secret clues." [*Clue of the Broken Locket*]

When surfeited with reading, I'd hold pretend conversations with Nancy or with Jo in *Little Women.* Sometimes, I'd groom Black Beauty, but more often would just stare out the window.

Surrounded by a winter in the glassed-in winter-garten, I gazed for hours at the falling snowflake doilies, dagger-like icicles, and multi-colored beams that, bouncing off the ice, mirrored the winter sun. Jack Frost was like a Skinny Santa, coming at night and decorating the world with an ominous purity. His new ice became skating rinks, and although he sometimes slipped, he never fell like people did. When Jack slipped, he just giggled and dreamed up another ice design. That's why every new snowfall looked different, and why people sometimes got hurt and needed to be careful. It was the different design that tripped them up.

In the spaces between reading and gazing, I made up another horse, not black but white, to help me be careful and keep Black Beauty company. Gabral was strong and had kind, gentle, horse eyes. Gabby frolicked almost unseen on the snow. When I let him in, he would neigh and nuzzle me, protecting me from the dark places in the house, those places where it felt as if sad people still lived. When night fell, Gabby had to leave or he would be spotted against the dark. A shadowy older girl named Pam, whom I couldn't quite "see" would appear and lead Gabral out. Later on, Pam would appear at odd times when Gabby wasn't around, and we would chat. I did most of the talking.

Mommy and Daddy were always busy. Still sometimes Mommy noticed I was behind in my lessons and get mad. "What do you do all day?" she'd ask. "Where's Irmgard?"

I'd shrug. "In school, I guess."

"And that's where you should be." Then she would tell me how I had to do the Calvert Course lessons.

"They're so *boring,*" I would say.

"How are you going to know what you're good at, if you don't try? You need to try different things—uncover your destiny." Sometimes, she'd tousle my hair. Usually, I didn't reply, but one time I said, "I'm good at reading."

Then Mommy frowned and pulled herself up into her stern position. "Your father and I have to go to Frankfurt for several days. When we get back, I want to see those lessons *done*, you hear me?"

"Yes, Ma'am," but she didn't tell me which lessons, so how could I do them?

The Christmas gingerbread house that had so surprisingly appeared had been set on a massive grand piano. Because of that, the gleaming piano held promise and one day, as I passed it, I realized I *was **already** good at something besides reading—music! I won two-and-a-half silver dollars at a piano recital once, not first prize but close, for playing "Three Trolls." Miss Coles, the music teacher said she was proud of me; Miss Coles, who did high kicks and Al Jolson imitations—had bent down and kissed me! Such a famous woman kissed me. Imagine!*

I slid the piano bench from underneath the piano, sat down and tried to play the *"Three Trolls"* but once past the initial trill, I couldn't recall the keys, but as I fumbled, my fingers remembered *"The Happy Hippo,"* my first piano piece. Those notes came as easily as breathing, and as they did, I sang, *"The Happy Hippopotamus you all must know/ a beast of a giant size/ the happy hippopotamus you must know/ he winks his strange little eyes. And oh...."*

Emmy strode into the living room wiping her hands on a dishtowel, her face peaked with interest. At first she stood impassive, listening. "Yah," she nodded, and then went back to the kitchen. Thrilled with her approval, I sang louder, my spirits lifting with each line and note. *"The happy hippopotamus at dawn plays in a giant pond/ he needs no magic wand / but oh his massive mouth...."*

After all, wasn't I in Germany, land of famous musicians, Beethoven, Chopin, and Bach? Now I had the answer to an unspoken question. Music was the reason I was in Germany, to learn in the land of the masters. My destiny was now uncovered.

"Mommy," I asked when my parents returned from Frankfurt, "Will you get me music lessons? I want to take music lessons."

Her eyebrows lifted, and her eyes widened. "Music lessons? This *is* a change." She cocked her head to one side as if trying to figure out something. "You never wanted to practice before."

"But I do now! Remember? Miss Coles said I was talented and had potential, but I had to practice, practice. If I did, I could get *really* good, maybe win first prizes. I could practice here, Mommy." I patted the piano. "I can still play 'The Happy Hippo.' Want to hear me?"

"Sure," but Mommy stood very still; her brow furrowed. I waited and waited for her to speak or nod.

"Shall I play now, Mommy?"

"The problem is, I don't know anyone who could teach you." She twisted her handkerchief.

How could she not know any music teachers in Germany, land of famous composers? There must be loads of them. A strange void appeared, a space without meaning. My stomach thudded. How could she demand I find my destiny, then not let me fulfill it? Memories of what she'd said about the sergeants flooded back. What was wrong with that woman?

Then I didn't realize that Mommy was right. How would she have found a German music teacher, one who spoke English, would teach without fear and not cause a diplomatic ruckus? Germans were hunkering down in response to the Occupation and to the "red menace." Because of their opposing ideologies, Germany's division, the Berlin Blockade and NATO, Russia and the Allies were at loggerheads. The Allies believed Russians would invade and seize Krupp industries, because during the war, they'd come and gotten a secret formula from Krupp for some kind of steel. In December 1950 Daddy wrote his mother:

The situation here with respect to a possible attempt by Russia on Western Germany is so serious.... There is as yet no force here sufficient to hold.... We are in the heart of the Ruhr where are the bulk of the coal and iron resources of Europe and... this is perhaps the first sector that the Russians would attempt to take and as we are a considerable distance on the wrong side of the Rhine we here feel particularly vulnerable.

It is well understood that if the Russians move, the only thing to do is for everyone to climb at once into their cars and race for the nearest bridge across the Rhine. Most of the bridges across the

Rhine were destroyed during the war and few have been rebuilt....
Probably these bridges would not stand long as they would be
sabotaged by communist sympathizers seeking to trap the allied
forces on this side or closed...

***

Still smarting from the pre-war communist fear and their
defeat by the Russians, particularly humiliations like the Battle of
Leningrad and the mass rape of Berlin women by Russian soldiers,
Germans went on red alert when Russians were mentioned.
Irmgard's father used to joke that I was a "Red," when I wore my
red dresses. Once Herr Prusnat asked me if Daddy could protect
"das kleinest mann" from "the reds."

So when Mommy twisted her handkerchief, she must have
been considering the diplomatic consequences of hiring a German
teacher. Hiring domestic help was all that was allowed, and even
then one was taking a chance; servants, or anyone, might be a
soviet spy. I had heard all this, but didn't connect it with my own
needs.

***

So, destiny thwarted, I lost interest in playing the piano, just
continued to wander about the house, devour books in the winter-
garten, and play with Irmgard when she showed up.

***

Something happened at Villa Hugel that upset Daddy and
distracted Mommy from almost everything. Still Mommy did *not*
forget the Calvert Course. Periodically, she ordered me to do those
lessons *or else!* But she never said what the "or else" would be.

So I tried but couldn't answer questions about the Constitution
or the Senate or much of anything about the government. Who was
the Speaker of the House? Weren't there more speakers than just
one in the whole House of Representatives? Also, arithmetic had
graduated into double numbers with a slash, like 7/21. What could
someone do with *that?* Every now and then I asked for help.
Daddy would help with one, then be gone. Mommy said she was

hopeless in math. Emmy said to "work, work," and that eventually I would figure out the answer. But I didn't do either one.

Instead, I took up candle-wax watching. Alone in the massive dining room with Calvert Course lessons spread before me, I lit candles. At first, I just wanted to revel in their glow and the patterns dripping wax made on the holders, always different, like snowflakes. Then I found that if I held candles at angles and dripped on left-over lunch plates, curious puddles would result, puddles I could change. If I didn't like the shape, I could shove it with a toothpick or match, reshape it, as long as I worked quickly before the wax hardened. First, I made a design like an *M* on the Calvert Course Covers which sealed up the whole thing, just like kings used to close important letters. Later I wanted to make more complicated designs, but couldn't seem to do it. Once I tried to make a two-tiered cake plate like I'd seen in a shop once. But the toothpicks I used as "pillars" broke when I put the hardened wax circles on them, and the whole structure fell, crumbling the carefully constructed "tiers" into candle bits. It was like the piano lessons or the math—I could get a little way into them, but no farther. Still, I stayed fascinated by the variations of the dripping wax and couldn't get enough of the flames.

After a time, the flames' white light and orange cores seemed to beckon me into them, into a different universe. What would it be like to be in the center of a Candle World, all bright like the snow, looking out at people as I looked out of winter-garten windows? I'd test myself by seeing how close I could hold the candle without getting burned. Sometimes I would stare so at the candle I was holding that it burned down and scorched my fingers. I also liked match flames, but that was unproductive and risky. I nearly always burned myself and then, of course, ruined the match. Matches had to be strictly rationed so no one would notice any missing. If I heard someone coming, I hid everything, especially the matches, and pretended to study. At night I would think about flames, candle flames, fireplace frames, gas flames, furnace flames, bon-fires.

But one afternoon, Emmy caught me. "Are you Stwelpeter?" She yanked the box of matches from the dining table and ran a hand over curled, burned scraps. I had burned paper to make the flames whoosh up. "What's this? Black—ashes? For what?" She stared at the wax-laden plates, plates I'd gotten from the cabinet no one used. "Gut Gott! I'll never get them off." She picked up a plate but some wax spilled on the tablecloth stuck the two together. "Mine Gott! Varoom?"

"Pretty designs," I said. "I'm making Mommy presents."

"What? . . . Mutter? . . . You'll burn us all up!"

"Yes, a surprise, but I won't do it again, I promise. Not if it makes you mad."

Emmy shifted the plates to her other hand and cuffed me hard on the ear. "Don't cover mit lies." As she left, the dishes she carried clanked against the enormous keys hung on her apron's sash.

With toothpicks, I picked at the candlewax on the tablecloth. Now Emmy would lock up the pantry, so it would be harder to steal matches. She would recognize the plates I'd filched and inspect the unused china cabinets. The best option was Daddy's matchbooks; he wouldn't notice if his matchbooks disappeared. But those didn't work as well as kitchen matches. I couldn't/ wouldn't give up my flames. Somehow, they warmed a cold spot inside me.

Emmy wasted no time telling Mommy my crime, who got very excited, especially when she discovered that most of my Calvert Course had burned. I overheard her tell Daddy that she wanted to send me to a special kind of Army doctor, but Daddy said there wasn't one in Essen, only Frankfurt, which was too far away. At dinner, she had red eyes, like she was mad or had been crying. Although she didn't say much of anything, I felt uneasy, like things were going to change.

A couple days later, Mommy invited Mrs. Merilees for tea without Dawn, which was a relief. No matter how I tried, when Dawn came, she would do something horrible, like open the oven door and put her finger in Emmy's rising bread to make it fall or pull down her pants and tell me she left worms wherever she sat. "You'd better watch where you sit, or they will get into *you.*"

Usually it was Mrs. Merrilees who phoned Mommy to see if she could help. She had decided to "help" after my horseback riding fiasco. We were the "singular" Americans, and Mrs. Merrilees thought it her duty to help us adjust. The conversation usually got around to Roger Merrilees who had something to do with Villa Hugel. Mrs. Merrilees would tell Mommy, "Roger can always get round matters." Then she would lift her chin. "But *I* manage Roger." Then she would tell how Roger would say something was "impossible," but she would make him do it anyway.

Usually Mommy and Mrs. Merrilees' chat was a kind of dance that began with Mommy's asking advice and ended with Mrs. Merrilees' giving it. Mommy's quandary was like a curtsy, and Mrs. Merilee's advice like taking Mommy's hand and royally lifting her up. My behavior often began the dance.

"I dress Mary Hanford in a clean dress every day and comb her hair until she cries. She leaves home looking like a lady, but comes back filthy, her hair a rat's nest. Your Dawn always looks so neat. How *do* you do it?"

"Well, I don't know about that, but certainly, Dawn knows about appearances." Mrs. Merrilees would sniff the air. "Perhaps Mary Hanford attended a school without *standards*. I know nothing about American schools, you understand, except they are obliged to let anyone in.

Yes, Dawn knew about "appearances." Dawn had made *me* climb the tree, not her, she made *me* approach a bee hive and suffer a bee attack, but I never snitched on her, not even when she lied about the missing pudding.

So when I heard that Mommy had invited Mrs. Merilees on her own, I worried. Once Emmy had served tea, Mommy closed the door. I hid in a broom closet with the door cracked, trying to hear but heard only voices. Once, Mommy coughed and choked, and I heard Mrs. Merilees pat her on the back. "There, there." When the door finally opened, I saw Mommy had that same red face as a few nights before. Mrs. Merilees stood up. "Never mind." She drew on her gloves, "We will sort it out." As she left, she pinched my cheek.

***

The next night Mommy came to my bedroom to tuck me in. That was unusual. She sat on the edge of my built-in bed and said she had a wonderful surprise for me: I was going to school, to the British school, only thirty kilometers away. A bus, or truck, was supposed to pick me up.

"But how? It's for Official British."

Mommy waved her hand. "Never mind that, dear. We worked it out." Mommy bent over and kissed me. You'll love it. "After all, it's Dawn's school!"

Yeah, right. Dawn.

Chapter Eight

Rule Britannia

I. A tuppence or a "whatence"?

Getting caught with my candles made such a fuss, there was no way I could escape going to the British school. My first indication that life there would be different from life on Elasse Str. occurred when a muddied military truck, driven by a crinkly British soldier, showed up late morning to take me to school.

My first day I was late because some papers had to be filled out. I didn't care about being late or going alone, because sunshine had started inside me. At school would be other kids, so I wouldn't have to put up with Dawn or entice Irmgard to come over. At school would be activities at set times and tasks. As the truck bumped over pot holes and squished through mud, I recalled new notebooks, school folders, crayons, the smell of library paste and the feel of yellow pencils all shiny and sharp the first days of school.

Except for being "careless" and talking too much, I'd always done well in school. It was mostly easy and fun—even getting caught talking was fun. The teacher would scold but smile at the same time.

Finally, the truck pulled into a large gate to a dirty white house with brown streaks running down the side. Deep woods surrounded this so-called school; we seemed way out in the country. Nestled in the woods were low, concrete buildings, which I supposed were doghouses, only with curved roofs. There were no swings or jungle-gyms. *Did they put them away because of the rain?* And no school traffic directors.

"Ready, Luv? Don't dawdle, and mind the steps." The driver jumped out and held out his hand to help me down, but I didn't take it.

Inside the dirty white house was a hall with coat pegs on one wall, and rooms branching off the hall. Close to the back wall was a staircase, like a backstairs in a fancy house. I started to go into one of the rooms but the driver stopped me.

"School's on first floor, Luv." He pointed to the staircase.

"This is the first floor."

"Sorry. This is the ground floor. Come on now, up the stairs with you."

I hesitated. How come the second floor was the first floor to the Brits? You'd think a second floor would be a second floor everywhere. As I followed the driver up the stairs, fear crawled in me.

A square woman was standing at the head of the stairs. Her body was square and beige as was her pale, unlipsticked face. Her brown short hair was square cut, like Buster Brown., and she wore a beige blouse and dark brown skirt which fell past her knees. Thick wool stockings covered oblong legs and thick ankles. She did not smile.

"Here, Miss Sutton, is the American, safely delivered. Found her out on Elasse Str.—made sure no Jerry got her." The driver doffed his beret.

"Right. I learned of her this morning—curious, actually. Never mind—well done. That will be all. Thank you." She nodded to the driver

The driver bowed and left.

"Well, Mary, we must get acquainted." She put her hand on my shoulder. "Your father works at Villa Hugel, runs the coal commission, right?"

"Well, he does something about Krupp."

"Really? Well, I suppose they are linked. Do you know what the coal commission does?"

"Not really. Something to do with heating people's places."

"Well, we have our work cut out for you, don't we? The coal commission is the board of directors that tries to keep Germans warm, despite the bombed mines. You may find it not so warm here, despite your father's position. We are still on rations."

Our house was always warm. So was Villa Hugel.

"Cat got your tongue? It's 'Yes, Miss.'"

"Yes, Miss Sutton," I replied.

"'Yes, Miss,' will be sufficient." *Why did it have to be just "Miss?" Wouldn't just "Miss" lead to confusion with the other teachers?* Then I didn't know Miss Sutton was the only real teacher.

"That's better; come along now." Miss Sutton propelled me towards the open door of the classroom, where we stood facing a big room with tables and about thirty kids of different ages. A big blackboard stood at the far end of the room and to the side of the blackboard sat the only desk, a regular teacher's desk. Three of the tables were long, like picnic tables; they even had benches. The fourth table was square, with two old rickety chairs, pulled up to it.

The students appeared to be working, but they were also talking, yet quietly. The class had a hum, not a roar.

"Class, attention, please." She boomed "attention" but said "please" softly.

"This is our new student, Mary, an American, a little exception to our policy. Perhaps she will prove "the exception that proves the rule." A slight smile slid across her face. Some of the older students tittered. I knew immediately I had worn the wrong thing.

"I'm confident you will show Mary the best of British culture. "Miss Sutton lifted her head and stuck out her chest like a soldier at attention. "Mary, you'll sit at that table near the window for now." Miss Sutton pointed to the empty square table with the rickety chairs. I went to the square table and perched on a seat with broken caning and hoped someone else would come. After all, there were two chairs.

I looked around. The kids didn't have nice clothes like mine, and they were all thin. There were no desks, lockers, folders or even any pencils. Students were writing with pens, real pens! Each student had a bottle of ink, like the ones Daddy used to fill up his fountain pen. They would dip their pens into the ink and then write; sometimes ink would puddle on the paper and they'd blot it with some thick, fuzzy-looking paper.

"Miss Sutton, I need a new nib," one student called

"Prefect will fetch it for you," Miss Sutton said, who was at her desk reading a paper.

What was "nib"? What was "prefect?" A tall girl, about fourteen, got up from her table and went to a cabinet; she brought out a key and unlocked it, then fiddled around with a box Then she locked the cabinet and brought the "nib" to the student, then came over to me.

"Here's your composition book, your pen, nib and ink." She plopped them down on the table. The only strange object was the pen point, so that had to be the nib.

"Might as well get started," she went back to her table. *Get started at what?* I didn't dare ask about crayons.

***

It turned out that those long, oblong tables meant something, depending on where they were placed. The one nearest Miss Sutton's desk meant "Academic," the one in the center of the room meant "Average," and the one in the back near the door meant "Working class." Wasn't the whole class working? Kids laughed when I asked that, but no one explained anything.

The square table was for those "in transition," as Miss Sutton put it. I sat at that table for almost a month. There I was supposed to listen, recite and write lessons, which seemed to have no particular order. Miss Sutton would present a lesson in history, grammar, reading, math, or science at the blackboard. Then she would give an assignment, which involved recitation and writing. Recitation meant answering her question in class. If we had trouble with an assignment, we were to find someone to help.

I paid attention to the lessons because I was isolated and close to the blackboard. Also I could get my questions answered easily because I was close to Miss Sutton. All this led to a fascination with English kings and queens, the Magna Carta struggle, old fights and monks writing things down in gold letters. Miss Sutton also talked about the war, but not about American superheroes or Nazis. Instead, she taught about battles the British fought. One of them was the Battle of Dunkirk. Seemed that soldiers were trapped by Germans in a French place called Dunkirk. The British decided to rescue them but didn't have enough soldiers left to do it, so they asked civilians to help, and bunches of little boats crossed the sea despite the German planes bombing them and rescued over three hundred thousand soldiers.

This was an impressive story, but Miss Sutton had left out some things. I raised my hand. "Yes, Mary Hanford? You have a question?"

"Yes, Miss. Where was the American air force?"

Again there was a general titter. "Mary Hanford, the Battle of Dunkirk occurred in 1940, May 26-June 4, to be exact. Your country didn't even enter the war until over a year later."

"Oh." I felt guilty, even though the battle had happened before I was born.

"At any rate, during the time row boats, skiffers, yachts, sail boats, and small fishing boats were crossing the channel to rescue the allies, a great fog occurred and blurred the vision of the Luftwafe."

Luftwhat?

"Some people believe that God sent that fog to protect us from Nazi detection. That is why one often hears that battle referred to as the "Miracle of Dunkirk." Certainly, it was a miracle that we succeeded, but on another level people believe that God intervened to save us."

I hadn't known any of this, even what the word "miracle" meant. I knew only that Germans were bad and Americans were heroes. From Miss Sutton, I inferred that "miracle" had to do with something unusual happening and God's doing part of it. The "something" might be a person who was supposed to die for sure, but didn't. You could prove that it happened, but not that God made it happen. So what was the use of God, then—as an excuse for weird things?

Because I had no one to chatter with at the square table; I listened and did well in most subjects. Despite the pen and ink blunders which resulted in blots on my pages and stains on my clothes, several "well-dones" appeared on my papers, even one "excellent." I dreamed of being at the "Academic" table, where kids actually discussed subjects, such as King Henry IV.

But when Miss Sutton ordered "Get out your maths book," I squinched down, hoping to hide. I was bad in "math." In Atlanta, fourth-grade fractions and word problems had petrified me. I blanked at problems such as "If Farmer Jones sells a dozen eggs for 50 cents and makes a profit of 33 1/3 percent, for how much does Farmer Jones have to charge to make 50% profit?"

So far, in Germany, I hadn't had to worry. Our family and everybody I knew in Essen used American "script," a kind of fake dollar used in the occupied zones. "Script" was just like dollars but printed funny. I also knew that there were four "marks" to the dollar and a hundred pfenings to the mark, just like a hundred cents to the dollar.

However, in this school, I was to learn how to add, subtract, and divide something called pounds, shillings, pence, halfpennies, and farthings. Halfpennies ("hay-pennies" they called them) were half a pence and farthings were one-fourth of a pence. Fourteen pence to a shilling also threw me; why wasn't it ten like other currencies? When I saw these fractions translated into money, I panicked. I tried hard, but despite help from older students, the prefect and sometimes Miss Sutton herself, I couldn't get it five minutes after help had left. Sometimes I'd be sure that I had it right, but when the class checked the math, I'd be wrong.

So despite shining in literature and history, Miss Sutton placed me at the average table. *That table was the biggest and had the most kids. I could never get along with all those kids.*

"But I do well in literature and history, Miss. I would improve more at the Academic table. They talk about assignments, not just do them. Even if I were just a Social Promotion, I would learn more."

"A *what* kind of promotion?" Her eyes slid down her nose and landed on me.

"'Social promotion,' you know—when the student really doesn't know the material but is promoted for his social good, for his adjustment."

"Good Lord, what rubbish! Gather your things Mary Hanford. Proceed to Table Two *now*." She jerked her head like she had just heard a siren warning.

I wanted to cry but didn't dare. At this school, one carried on, despite injustice, despite hardship, maybe especially hardship. Complaining—about anything—was not "good form."

"Carry on," or "Never mind," Miss Sutton would say, no matter how hard the rain came through the roof, how long the taps froze, how cold the school was or how many days when she announced that no lunch would be provided.

As if in defiance of adversity, Miss Sutton would pull herself up and thrust out her ample bosom and begin lessons of valor. "King Henry, you recall…." Her manner and her lessons indicated that the British were superior beings. When conditions were particularly bad, she would repeat the story of the "miracle" at Dunkirk. That a Higher Being would deign to create fog so British boats could cross to Dunkirk without being detected indicated that this Higher Being considered the British worthy, and thus would likewise get them through any crisis.

Despite holes in clothes, sniffles, sneezes, and coughs, one carried on. I soon discovered that any whining on my part was not tolerated.

"It's freezing in here. Why isn't there a heater?"

"You think you're the bloody queen!" someone would snap.

Although complaining was not allowed, speaking up was permissible, so I continued to protest. "But I can do better…." I repeated.

"Prove it." Miss Sutton turned back to the blackboard.

So I would. Somehow I would claw myself to the "Academic" table.

When Miss Sutton first brought me over to the Average Table, no one greeted me except to move over and murmur. I felt lost. I hadn't minded being alone at the square table that much, for I was used to being alone and I caught Miss Sutton's attention more easily. None of the kids interacted with me much except to borrow blotting paper or ask a question, so I didn't speak to them either— just did my work. But I listened to them talk, mostly about each other. Dawn was especially keen on belittling people's accents, saying certain families weren't like "us, socially." Gordon, the boy who might be riding with me sometimes, bragged about his father. His friend Donald always told him not to "swank."

Many times I didn't know what they were talking about. Whoever told me that the British were like Americans was wrong. Once Miss Sutton mentioned a message on the "wireless."

"What is a wireless?" I asked and the kids bent over with muffled laughter.

"Clearly, Mary Hanford, by putting two and two together, you can solve this for yourself. I was speaking of messages from England, from the BBC? Do you see any BBC people here?"

I shook my head, although I had no idea what or who BBC was."

"Now, if there is no evidence of BBC here, where would I get their messages?"

"Oh, a radio."

"Precisely."

A few at the Average Table seemed really interested in some subjects. Pale, asthmatic Anne read King Arthur books that she'd stashed under the table. When we were supposed to be doing something else, sometimes she would pass me a book and whisper to me not to worry. Lucinda liked hearing about the war, how glorious the British were. Her father wasn't in Essen, but her mother worked at Villa Hugel.

At recess kids asked questions, which I couldn't answer, such as "What's your father's rank?" "Why do you get to live in Heisingen?" and "Why are you here in *our* school?"

"Coo—look at that skirt. Ain't she posh?" Charlotte snickered.

"What's posh?" I threw out. More laughter.

"It's not just 'posh' she doesn't know. Ask her what 'jumper' means or 'garter' or 'loo'"

They laughed and poked each other, getting red in the face.

"Loo. She'd better find that out. Ha-ha."

Finally Anne broke in. "Well, why should she know? She's from a foreign country."

"And she doesn't curtsey to grown-ups, proper grown-ups, not servants," Dawn went on.

"Why don't you?" Anne asked.

"I didn't think I had to. We don't do that in the States."

"So—no respect for position. That's what I've heard," Gordon said.

"You bloody Americans think you're better, but you aren't!—you're selfish. You didn't help us until you were hurt," Donald chimed in.

"Did not!"

"Did too! My dad told me, and he's a colonel."

"No!" Americans were heroes. "We saved you."

"Saved yourselves in the doing," Donald snapped. I was stumped, so didn't answer.

"So what's your dad? Higher than a colonel?" Gordon asked.

"I don't' know," I said. More laughter but then stillness.

"Then *why* are you here? This is a school for British, state and military, mainly for the coal commission." Gordon twisted his face, as if puzzled.

"I didn't do my Calvert Course."

"Your what?"

"Yah, she's here because she's daft, likes fire," Dawn broke in. "Mum's afraid she will burn the house down, so sent her here to burn down our school instead, ha, ha!"

The inquisition stopped; everyone brightened up. "Burn down the school? Great!"

"Yes, burn it down—ha, ha, ha," Gail cheered. "No more Sutton, no more canes."

"No more whip-stinging pains," Lucinda chanted.

"No more slipping on muddy lanes," Fiona chimed in.

Then the prefect rang a cow bell, and we all ran back into class.

When school let out, and we were all running out of class, a boy yelled, "Burn it up, Mary. Burn it! Burn it *all* up!" Others laughed with him, and I felt the mood change.

II. The Queen's Creed, One Smack at a Time

I hadn't been there a month when language again caused me trouble. Miss Sutton had announced there had been a "directive." Instead of regular classes, for a week, we were to be taught religion, "which we all know is necessary for any civilized society." She introduced a dumpy girl, Melanie, who would explain matters, as soon as we were sorted out. We were to meet in a downstairs room first thing in the morning.

The next day, in a cavernous room cluttered with boxes stamped with the British crest, we lined up before a desk that was really stacked boxes. When my turn came, I was baffled.

"Church of England or Roman Catholic?" Miss Sutton had an enormous pen in her hand and an equally huge bottle of ink beside a small writing tablet.

"I don't know"

"You don't *know*?" She pursed her lips and squinted at me. Miss Sutton smelled like camphor; that's probably why she squinted. It was strong, even for her.

I shook my head. But I knew I wasn't Catholic "I'm not Roman Catholic. My parents are Athiens." Miss Sutton looked at Melanie. The Aide chuckled then put her hand over her mouth.

"Church of England, then." Miss Sutton marked something beside my name.

"What? I'm an American."

"Go on with you then, left side of the room." From her head jerk towards the left side, I knew I'd just better go. Besides, most of the kids were on that side. Across the room were only a few students; Roman Catholics, I guessed.

***

The next day we sat in a circle with Melanie who had a book called *The Book of Common Prayer*. We were to memorize and recite it to Miss Sutton.

"Now, altogether students; repeat after me. 'We confess that we have sinned in what... blah-blah... and there is no health in us....we are not worthy to pick up the crumbs under thy table...." *What table?*

"Now the Creed." Melanie cooed lots of long words "'...Resurrection of the body and the holy catholic church'" I told Melanie that I thought being Catholic and Church of England were different. If they weren't, why did we have to choose and line up on both sides of the room?

"They are different. The queen wants us to learn about the Church of England because she is Head of the Church."

"I thought God was head of the church. Besides, my parents are Athiens."

"God IS the head but so's the queen. Didn't you *hear* the queen on the wireless? She wants every British person to know the creed."

"What's the creed?" I whispered to Gordon.

"What you've got to learn, Stupid!"

"But *what* is it?"

Gordon scratched his head. "Dunno, really."

"And what's a wireless?"

Gordon slapped his forehead. "Oh, God, you don't remember *anything?*"

"I do too!"

"Do not, do not." Dawn and Fiona chimed in with Gordon.

"Athiens, her parents are Athiens." Dawn pointed at me.

"Straighten up now! See this bit, the 'quick and the dead?' You'd better learn this quick or you'll be dead when Miss finds out," Melanie said.

Someone rang the cow bell for recess, and Dawn pushed past me laughing, "Athiens, Athiens. Creed, Greed....!"

"You bums!" I yelled, even before I got my coat.

Melanie stopped on the stairs. "Bums?" She frowned. "I'm going to get Miss. You can't be allowed."

Miss came down to the cavernous room and brought me back upstairs. She had her willow branch with her. "Is it true that you called the others bums?"

"They were mean to me, so they *are* bums. They're *all* bums, bums!"

"We'll see what happens to your 'bum' when it's thrashed! I won't tolerate a filthy mouth!" Smack!

And so that's how I really learned British English, one smack at a time.

II. Fairy Rings and Willow Canes

After that, I turned inward. If I were quiet and didn't cause trouble, maybe I'd be left alone; by being quiet I could just look around, observe, and read. I had read Anne's King Arthur's book and was reading about the "wee folk" and "fairies" in Ireland, but could only do that in off times. It wasn't only the kids that upset me; what bothered me almost more was how ugly and lean everything seemed.

One day I was looking at the lunchroom walls trying to avoid the food. The walls were a dirty yellow—maybe white once. On my plate was an ice cube of meat with fat all around it and a puddle of green stuff. I asked once what the green stuff was.

"Peas, Stupid," Dawn said.

Mommy said the British were still on rations, but I never saw *any* rayon stockings. Miss Sutton wore thick, wool stockings. The kids wore wool, knee socks. But maybe I'd forgotten some stuff because I was only five when Mommy had to wear "Damn war rations," rayon stockings.

That day we had dessert, a saucer of pudding called Blank Mange. It had chocolate and vanilla swirls, pretty, like skirts swirling. If I didn't eat the fat stuff and the pea gravy, Miss would take away the Blank Mange. The only way I could get the fat chunk down was to wash it down with the green stew. So I did and then dipped into the Blank Mange, but ugh! It wasn't chocolate or vanilla—or anything! It tasted like the library paste I'd eaten in kindergarten.

"Stop dawdling," Miss said, "can't you see the others have gone?" They were mingling in the hall, waiting for recess. Then the bell clanged and kids rushed out onto the concrete pavement scuffling and screaming because it had stopped raining. I ran too—ran so they would think I had someplace to go. I did—those woods where Ann swore were fairy rings. The woods looked like they even had dwarves.

We're weren't allowed in the woods, so I stayed on the schoolyard's edges looking at the concrete doghouses with the curved roofs that people called "Bunkers." After a while, I looked back and saw boys kicking a soccer ball. The girls sat in a circle, maybe playing jacks. The prefect was talking to a boy, who was waving his arms about. No one missed me, so I slipped into the woods.

It was very wet. There were pine needles and low branches, which shook water on me if I brushed by. The trees were so tall; I couldn't see the tops. But there were also bushes, some with brambles and all loaded with water. Little things had sprouted up. Some of those were brown with caps, little caps curved under. Did they do that on purpose to make little umbrellas? I wanted to pick one, but remembered that these could be toadstools and poisonous. But were they poisonous if someone just touched and smelled them? They looked slimy but didn't smell. I heard a sudden noise and jumped. I looked up to see two squirrels dart up a tree. One went way up, and the other ran onto a small branch, which bent and dripped more water on me. He looked at me, chattered and waved his tail. "Go away," he seemed to say.

So I left and tromped over wet brown leaves and tiny sticks. Sometimes the leaves and sticks were matted together like in a fairy's hut. Maybe I was close to a fairy ring. It was a relief to be alone with the trees, which have souls like we do, the Druids said.

I didn't want to go back to those kids or Miss Sutton. If I found a fairy ring, maybe the fairies would help me. I started going sideways and suddenly saw splotches of color. An animal, flowers? I crept up and found a circle of tall toadstools, with big wide tops that are red, red with white polka dots. They didn't curve but stuck right out. Their stalks were whitish, like celery. I got on my knees to look under their big polka dot hats. Something scraped and hurt, but I didn't care. Underneath their hats was webby stuff, tiny veins, a kind of netting. Veils for the hats? Did the fairies wear the tops for hats? They were in a circle, not scattered like the brown ones. Why? To take care of something, to protect it? That's what fairies did; they protected, left presents. Then these toadstools were a fairy ring! So I stepped into the middle of the circle and waited. A long time. No fairies came. A screech sounded and I jumped up and saw a big brown bird flying from one high branch to another. Then again, the cow bell. Recess was over.

As I passed the grey curved things, I looked inside one. It smelled bad, like something rotten. If it hadn't smelled, it would have been a good place to hide because it was too big for a dog. But Miss Sutton would catch me.

No one was on the playground. Suddenly, I was cold as well as wet. My knees were scratched. Dirt and leaves dotted my skirt and stickers stuck in my cardigan. As I went through the door I noticed my coat dangling by its collar on the hook and knew I was in for it. I had tried to get it but was squished by the kids roaring past, so couldn't. That's what I decided to tell Miss Sutton anyway.

The stairs creaked, even though I was tiptoeing. Near the top I saw Miss Sutton's brown lace-up shoes, the bottom of her black skirt, and the tip of her flexible willow stick. I was going to be caned.

"Where have you been, Mary Hanford?" Miss Sutton shook my shoulders; the willow stick fell on the floor by her shoes with a soft click. "Class has been in session over ten minutes. I sent Prefect out to find you but she did not! Anything could have happened to you. The war may be officially over, but it really isn't. Someone could hurt your father through hurting you. It's post-war. Do you understand?"

I didn't understand but was too frightened to say so. Miss Sutton's voice reminded me of the radio announcer during air raids, just after a siren. "Go now to the shelter. Go *now."*

"Where were you? I asked you a question. Look at me!" Miss Sutton's voice was low, like an approaching storm.

"I was in the woods, Miss. I went to the woods to find fairy rings."

"The woods! You're forbidden to go the woods. Fairy rings! Nonsense. Answer me!" She cocked her head in and stared, waiting.

"Miss, I'm not lying I wanted to find fairy rings." I wasn't sure she heard me because of her flashing anger-lightning.

"And what, may I ask, were you to do with these 'fairy rings'?"

"Well, I thought that they...ow!" The willow stick—snakelike in its surprise nimbleness—struck with a sudden snap and sharp sting. "Ow, ow!"

"No coat, unkempt, insubordination," she chanted, as she lashed. She pushed my back but I was already bent and braced. Again and again, the burning, first on my calves, then the stick whipped onto my thighs I bit my lip until the salty metallic taste of blood dribbled into my mouth. Miss Sutton's black skirt swayed as she pulled back the cane to whip it forward again. As the lashes on my leg flicked quick and hard, I resolved not to cry. Through my legs I could see that the stumps above her high topped lace-ups were like raw chicken legs, pale and dimply.

"And your shoes—ruined...no, NO coat! —Children, German children, even English children would steal for that coat—send their souls into bloody hell because of *your* wasteful carelessness."

Those words knifed me; I'd seen enough of cold, shivering Germans, Irmgard in her worn "best blouse," Krystal with no socks in the bitter cold, Emmy's threadbare coat that she wore to bed. My resolve not to cry crumbled, and I broke.

I turned and threw myself onto her; her camphor smell was mixed with sweat. "Yes, yes—sorry, sorry! I don't want them to be cold, don't want them to....snot ran down my nose. "Sorry," I squeaked.

Miss Sutton stood for a moment letting me clutch and sob. Then she pulled back and fastened a loose button on her cuffs and smoothed the starched white blouse my tears had spotted. "I should think so. Now you may return to school and carry on with geography, South India, Chapter Three." She put the willow stick back on the hall shelf. "I must have a word with Cook before History," she said and disappeared down the stairs. The hall clock said 2:30; what seemed like days had been only fifteen minutes.

I turned towards the classroom and saw Lucinda, Gordon and Anne bunched in the doorway, staring. Without saying anything, I rushed past them and somehow made it to my seat. Nobody else said anything either.

After school, in the usual scramble to get coats, I hung back so others could get theirs before I retrieved mine, no one would notice me. But as Gordon and Donald rushed by, Gordon yanked my hair.

"First caning, eh?" He said, smiling or smirking, I couldn't tell which.

""Now, you're a proper Brit, Girlie." Donald swaggered.

"And it's about bloody time, if you ask me." Gordon pulled his cap down over his eyes. And punched me in the arm. Then they both took off.

III. A Good Deal Less Taxing

After that caning, almost everybody (except Dawn) stopped taunting me. I got the hang of the politics of the "Average Table," and learned to handle the etiquette of pen nibs: when to lend them, when to give them, how to hide the nib trafficking so Miss Sutton didn't catch us. We were allowed only two nibs per semester, and they were doled out and kept track of by the prefect, who could be bought off with sweets. I no longer tried to distinguish myself academically, as it was important not to "swank" at my table, and I desperately wanted to fit in. I even ventured gossip, although spent most of the time listening to it.

As might be expected, my maths grade deteriorated even further—the assignments going the way of the Calvert Course. Miss Sutton suggested I drop my study hour and join the embroidery class to raise my overall grade.

"Mary Hanford, girls are not born to maths; maths are hardly ever girls' natural inclination." Miss Sutton patted my shoulder. "Embroidery, on the other hand, is as natural as breeding for girls, and a good deal less taxing." I was surprised, for I thought embroidery was only for grandmothers.

Embroidery class was held when the boys had "sport," and when I was usually being tutored. In embroidery the girls took the evenness of their bargello stitches and the size of their hoops seriously. So I did too. I never asked why we weren't playing soccer with the boys outside, or what we were to do with our embroidery projects once we'd finished. Embroidery seemed as useless as maths, but a lot more fun.

As Christmas time approached, and many embroidery students were also in choir, some came back early from lunch for Carol practice. I started going with them, and unofficially became a choir member. No one seemed to care. When the prefect or Miss was out, we belted out "When Angels washed their socks one night/all seated round the tub/the angel of the Lord came down/and taught them how to scrub," Parodying the Carols was great fun, and we laughed until we hurt the time British School Inspectors stepped in to tell us how much they enjoyed our "sacred music," as they made their rounds. Finally, even though my stitches weren't even and I couldn't do maths, I fit in.

In fact, I fit in so well, people stopped noticing me. My resolve to be quiet had backfired. I went from the lessons at the Average Table to embroidery, religion class and choir unremarked.

Once Miss Sutton called role and counted me absent, until I showed her I was present. Another time, Prefect looked in on our five-member study session and referred to "the four of you."

"I'm here! I'm here. That makes five!" I waved my hand.

"Oh, so you are," she said and disappeared.

Then, I felt not like an American nor like a Brit, but like a cipher, a zero—not even there.

School went on as usual, so did home. Miss Sutton was absorbed in grading; boys at my table wagered on soccer teams, and most girls did their lessons. Choir and Embroidery classes were reliefs. Outside was cold and muddy. Anne, Lucinda and I huddled together near the school door and pooled our ignorance about sex. Home also went on as usual with just me and Emmy. My parents were in Bruges. Herr Prusnat had gone to visit relatives he hadn't seen since the war and had taken Joey with him.

That week Emmy was on a cobweb and disinfectant rampage, clattering around the house, even at night, with brooms and stinky pesticides. In a pile of clothes on the floor, I found an old wool dress, covered in tiny woolen "pills." The stain-splotched skirt was hunter green; the bodice was a muted red with mismatched buttons. There was raggedy rip in the high neck, as if someone with a fat neck had pulled it on. Whoever gave it to Mommy thought it would fit me, because it was about my size in a Salvation Army sort of way. I decided to wear it to school to see if anyone would notice the change. It would be an experiment.

Monday, I put down the date and "dress," in my composition book to mark how long it would take for the dress to draw attention, what the comments would be. Four days passed, and no one commented at school or at home. Even Emmy didn't notice that I wore the red and green dress four days running, but then I always got myself ready for school.

Finally, Katy said, "Why don't you take off that sodden dress? We all know you have other clothes, lots of them."

"Yes, you've worn it all week!" Dawn snapped, evidently lying in wait for the right moment to attack.

"You think you're better than us and wear that dress over and over to make fun of us, but we're on to your game!" Katy continued.

"No, no," I blurted, but then class ended and we all filed out. But later I realized the experiment had worked, just not in the way I expected.

Was the experiment really over? Only one person, Katy, had noticed. Dawn had only chimed in. One person was pretty poor results for an experiment. I told myself that Edison failed over a hundred times before he invented the light bulb. So I decided to wear that dress the next week to see if anyone else commented.

I didn't have to wait long. Tuesday, right after embroidery, Miss Clayson, our embroidery teacher, who was really a milliner, motioned for me to stay after class.

"Are you aware that you *smell*, Mary Hanford, that the horrible dress you've been wearing two weeks stinks?"

"No, Miss—it can't be. I take a bath every night" I hoped I wouldn't get slapped.

"Mary Hanford, you don't smell like bodies! Bodies have a natural smell—this smell fouls the air now that we have to be so shut up."

So the wool had absorbed Emmy's pesticides, but I didn't say so. Emmy might get in trouble.

"I've made a report to Miss Sutton concerning your slovenly conduct. Nonetheless, I told her you were quite good in embroidery and that you have a fine color sense. Shall we go in and see her now?"

"Okay."

Miss Sutton was standing at her desk when we both walked in.

"Sit down, Mary Hanford. I know the situation and can smell it now. The odor is disgusting. What do you have to say for yourself?"

I blathered about how I was trying to implement the scientific method and how the experiment was a success but not the results I wanted because "Other variables entered in."

"But *why,* Mary Hanford, did you choose this "experiment" as you call it? Were you supposed to pollute our air, stifle us with insecticide? If so, who told you to do this? Is this a cold war matter, or did some German put it into your head?"

Miss Sutton's face scrunched, "What does your father *do* when he goes to Frankfurt; you're always telling us he is in Frankfurt, whereas I was told that he headed at Villa Hugel with the UK/US Coal Commission. That's the only reason we let you in, you know. And what about your mum? Does she go with him on these mysterious trips?"

I had lied about Daddy's always being in Frankfurt or Bremen. Neither of my parents came to conferences because I tore up all notes about parent/teacher meetings. I didn't want Daddy's showing up at school drunk.

"No, no one put me up to it, it's just that...I wanted, needed, someone—anyone—to notice me. I'll stop. I'll stop!" I snuffled, then collapsed into sobs. Even though crying was not good form, fear of being caught in lies broke me. My tears blurred Miss Sutton's grade book with big, splashy drops. She saw it, but said nothing. Both women stayed silent.

IV. Almost British

The next day in embroidery class, Miss Clayson asked me if I would like to join the Girl Guides.

"What's that?"

She explained that it was the British version of Girl Scouts. I would be a first level Brownie, but could work myself up with enough merit badges. Miss Clayson was what Americans called a "den mother" and could help me win merit badges, especially with my talent for embroidery. I would have to wear a uniform, and she could provide one about my size, but my parents would have to pay for it. Would I like to join?

"Yes, yes, please." I felt airborne. Someone, some group wanted *me!* It never occurred to me that they were trying to keep me out of trouble.

Whatever the staff's reasons, things got better. Like embroidery, Brownies was fun. I worked hard on my merit badges, using my embroidery skills to sew badges and make placemats for war orphans or amputees. Except for Anne and me, all the Brownies and Girl Guides were from the Academic table. But rank didn't seem to matter at Brownies. We all worked together, and I forgot about maths, stopped daydreaming and fretting that nobody except Emmy was hardly ever home. Because we were altogether, the troop became home.

The Brownies met twice a week for an hour after school. My uniform was exactly like other girls' and I even learned to sing "God save the Queen..." although that felt a little strange right after King George died. He died in February, so it was frigid, but the whole school went to ceremonies for him and there was a special place for the Brownie/Girl Guides troop. The ceremonies were outside, and it was freezing even for February and boring— just a bunch of military holding flags riding around on horseback. But I felt happy, even though it was a sad time. I was a British Brownie like the others, and I was at ceremonies for King George. I was almost British. When the service was over and we were filing out, a man in a black suit and top hat said, "Pretty bad business, eh what?"

"Quite." I sounded British to myself.

He nodded. "Well, we'll carry on, won't we, for George's sake?"

"Righto," I replied. He pinched my cheek and strode off.

By spring, most of us were almost ready to graduate into Girl Guides. I had earned almost enough merit badges and was working hard to finish the last one. Anne had earned all of hers and was helping me with mine. She had become my best friend, even though she had asthma and couldn't play much. Sometimes she panted so hard at recess that she was allowed to come inside. Then Anne read books on maths and on planets as well as King Arthur books. I had a few other friends: Katy, Lucinda, even Gordon— but none like Anne. But I didn't think about individual friends when I was with the Brownies, just reveled in being with the group.

I was biting off a piece of navy thread when Miss Clayson got out her measuring tape and called for us to come be measured for Girl Guide uniforms.

"We have to order them, you see, and it will take a long time to get them from London." She squinted through her glasses at a list she held in her right hand. "Susan Appleworth, come forward."

I went back to finishing the edges of the flower I was going to stitch onto a placemat. Miss Clayson's name calling faded into background music, until I heard her call "Gillian Edwards" and realized she had gone past the B's and my last name, Baldy. I had been so intent on sewing that I had missed it. I raised my hand. She looked up from her list.

"Yes, Mary Hanford?"

"Sorry, Miss, but I believe you missed me."

"I beg your pardon. I did not miss your name. Let us remember, Mary Hanford, that you are an American." Miss Clayson cocked her head and stared at me.

What? I didn't say anything but the 'what' showed in my face.

"So, as such, you couldn't become a full-fledged Girl Guide, could you?"

"Oh, I guess not."

"Right. You're a bright girl; I'm sure you understand." Miss Clayson's eyes smiled behind her glasses. She turned back to her list. "Amy Forsythe, come forward."

I was stunned. *How could I have known? No one told me. They would say I should have known this already, and they were right. I was an American and nothing would change that. How could I have been so stupid? Stupid stuff like this was why I would always be at the Average Table no matter how hard I tried. If I couldn't become a Girl Guide, then why did Miss Clayson invite me in the first place—to give me something to do? No, she invited me because she felt sorry for me. I could tell by her "Sorry-for-you-tone.* Suddenly, I felt empty, really empty, and wished I hadn't thrown away the extra sandwiches Mommy always made me carry. I started to rip out my stitches on the placemat.

"Don't; don't waste it. You've done marvelously on embroidery," Anne whispered and put her hand on my hoop.

I nodded but kept my head down because I didn't want to show how close I was to tears. I had cried too much already. "Those placemats will be a marvel. Please finish them." Anne's breath rattled softly. She was upset also, or she wouldn't be wheezing.

I looked up at Anne's round face—she was so very pale. She might drop dead any time. I couldn't bear to disappoint her.

"All right," I said, but deep down knew I never would.

V. Cast the First Stone

At home, over my 4 p.m. tea and cucumber sandwiches, I reflected on how wrong I'd been in thinking shabby dress could help me—these kids were diplomats' kids and they wore shabby clothes. My Garfunkel's clothes already had drawn attention, but not in a good way. Thinking shabby clothes would elicit sympathy was American thinking, sloppy thinking. Compared to the British, Americans were rich—and wasteful. No wonder they wouldn't let me become a Girl Guide. And I was one of the worst Americans, for I threw away the extra sandwiches Mommy made me bring. Extra sandwiches began because once I told Mommy that after lunch I was still hungry.

"Hungry? My God, why didn't you tell me? You poor baby!" Mommy clutched me.

"Emmy, come here please!"

From then on, every day Emmy had to fix a lunch for me to take in addition to the school's food. I was already chubby and the thought of having to eat a second lunch revolted me. But to Mommy, I was always only ounces away from starvation. Each day, Emmy, whose fiancé was *still* in Argentina, daily handed me a bag with two sandwiches, usually tuna, chips, graham crackers and two cartons of chocolate milk.

For a while, I hid the brown bags in the forest until Emmy got suspicious. "Why you not bring back leftover food. You waste food, you waste life," and she'd lower her thin face close to mine, her eyes fiery, implying Hellish consequences if I were wasteful.

And I was wasteful, a wasteful American. The experiment had proven that. What should I do about those sandwiches? I could give them away but there was not enough for all the kids or Miss Sutton and Melanie. Besides, they would think I was swanking. Then I thought of all those dank and cold bunkers. Like stone hedgehogs, they were all over the place. Nobody paid attention to them.

So I decided to invite Anne and Dawn to meet me in the bunker, to tell them it was a surprise but a *secret*, and that if they came, they couldn't tell *anyone!* I decided on Anne because she needed extra food, and Dawn because she was unpredictable, nice for a while and then terrible. After being terrible, Dawn would be sorry and promise never to do "it" again, but she always did. I had to get the upper hand, or at least an even hand with her. Maybe food would do it.

When I invited Dawn, she just sneered at me. "Secret. Haven't we been through this before? What kind of secret could *you* have?" She wrinkled up her nose at me.

But Anne showed up. Tall and gangly, she barely fit into the bunker. When I gave her a tuna sandwich, she gulped it like a starving dog. Then we divided the chips and graham crackers. That afternoon, I returned home with crusts and an empty potato chip bag. "Zer gut," Emmy said when she looked in the bag.

A day or two later, Dawn showed up claiming she only "Wondered where Anne had got to." When she plowed into the food, I knew I had her. Whenever Dawn threatened to pull my hair or spill ink across my compositions, I reminded her—sometimes with only body language—the banquet would close if she pulled anything.

Sometimes we hid cookies under heavy moss in the bunkers; always we knew that comfort was just a bunker away. Dawn got nicer, and Anne got meat on her bones. Bones—rhymes with stones. Meat rhymes with neat, and neat was the trick that Dawn pulled. I should have known better than to again try to best her.

Anne and I had just finished half the graham crackers, when we heard noise outside. We crunched down, expecting a teacher or prefect. Instead, Dawn poked her head inside. "Ah, here are the thieves and robbers."

We crawled out into a group of enraged students circled around the bunker; they looked crazed, particularly Jane; her skinny frame was ramrod stiff; her face pointed at us like a hunting dog's.

"Food, food—you bloody rich American—hiding food, showing favorites!" Jane yelled.

"We are not thieves," I yelled. Anne squatted behind me trying to hide, but she was taller, so didn't fool anybody. Anne's knee socks wrinkled as she huddled behind me.

"Where's the food? You've been having food all along and still eating ours. And not sharing the extras!" Jane's eyes were glazed.

"I wouldn't have thought you would hide food from *me.*" Gordon stared at the ground.

"It was supposed to be only for me. I wasn't supposed to give it to anyone. But it was too much. My mother is always afraid I will get hungry and would kill me if she knew I'd given *any* away. But there wasn't enough for everybody," I gasped.

"You're fat already," Jane spat. She flicked her jump rope out, slapped my leg, and then drew it in like a lasso.

Anne held out to Dawn the bag half-full of chips. Dawn took it, spit on the ground and then held out the bag to the others who clustered around her.

"See, Mary asked me to share her bounty, and I did once or twice. But my conscience bothered me—holding out on you. I would *never* do that." She threw a side glance at Anne.

"What a rotter you are, Anne. But I was never fooled by your saintly act." Dawn turned back to the others. "You can expect Americans to be greedy but not Brits. Anne hogged it all for herself!"

"Americans are not greedy! We saved you in the war! We're building with the Marshall Plan!" I screamed.

Jane's foot toyed with playground gravel.

"Calm down, Mary." Gordon stepped towards me, but I backed away; then so did he.

"You *are* greedy. You not only had your own food, you ate ours!" Jane's face twisted. She had picked up a rock. It occurred to me that Jane might have gotten hungry a lot; she was so bony. Her clavicles were small hills under her shirt; her legs, sticks.

"But I had to; they made my parents pay lunch money. What was I supposed to do, not eat anything? That would only get Miss angry."

"All year you complained about how you didn't fit in and were miserable, yet all that time eating our food just because your mum paid! Didn't you think of us, didn't you think we could have eaten more?" Lucinda's eyes bulged.

Gordon's sad tone rose into anger. "My father's sick of Americans swanking over us; he says your class depends on money, not standards. He's right!"

They had completely misunderstood my motives. I was beginning to feel righteous.

"It was only one tuna sandwich, and Dawn is the rotter! She ate for weeks, and then snitched. As for you, Gordon, you're just jealous, Gordon, no—your father is jealous; because we whipped the Germans and you Brits couldn't do anything but beg for our help!"

"Could too! Did too! My dad flew over Krupps' place and bombed the bloody hell out of it in February 1942. Got a medal for it he did. Your country didn't even enter the war until December. We'd been there from the start."

"Mine lost a leg in 1941. Now he just sits around," Lucinda said. That's why only Mum works for the commission."

"Uncle Robin was blown up just before the war ended, only four days before. Pity I never met him. He was Mummy's brother." Fiona looked at the ground.

"And what did your father do in the war? He's got all his arms and legs. He may be a big shot on the coal commission, but all I've ever seen him do is smoke cigarettes and drink with Tommys at Villa Hugel's red bar." Dawn's lips smacked into a thin line.

Mentioning Daddy's drinking tipped me into offense. I wanted to puncture that bloated superior sense.

"Oh, just shut up! What do you know about anything, especially my father? I'm sick of hearing about yours. I wish *all* your dads had been blown up, especially yours, Dawn, the potbellied, weak-brained Merrilees. Then it would be clear who the real victors are!"

At that, they all got quiet. Dawn's face went white.

"Oh, you do, do you—because you ate our food, you want our dads blown up." Gordon said

"Yes, every last one of them, blown to smithereens!"

"Go ahead, Jane. Do it," Gordon murmured.

"Do it!" somebody echoed.

Jane threw the rock. It hit Anne who fell to her knees and put her hands over her head, a gesture which seemed to egg on the others. Others picked up stones and started throwing them at us. I stood still as they pelted us, imagining myself St. Joan hearing angels while people burned me up. I kept trying to will myself not to feel or flinch.

"Rotter, Thief, Fatso," they yelled as they threw rocks, pebbles, anything. Gordon just leaned on a tree trunk.

"Ow!" I finally yelped, just as the cow bell clanged. Everybody ran towards the school.

***

When we got there we settled quietly into our spots. Miss Sutton patrolled the tables, a slight frown revealing her suspicion. We put on a good show of getting out books and composition books, testing pen nibs.

Finally Miss Sutton returned to her desk and stood before it. "Anne and Mary Hanford, you two are filthy and have a strange, hang-dog expression. Most unusual for you, Anne. Come here."

We processed to her desk, side by side.

"Anne, your stockings are shocking." Miss Sutton lifted Anne's skirt and saw her scratched legs. The red scratches on Anne's white legs looked like Miss Sutton's red ink corrections on paper. "Good Lord, what did you do to yourself?" Anne didn't answer. I glanced at her. Her eyes were sad, like Sid Wilner's when I last saw him.

Miss Sutton turned towards me. "Undoubtedly, you also have scratched legs. And there's also a scratch on your left temple. Mary Hanford, why are you hunching like that? Straighten up and come closer. Now turn round." She lifted up my skirt. "Hummph," she said and then lifted the hair on the back of my head

"Blood, Blood!" Miss Sutton almost shrieked. I felt there; it was sticky. "Right after history, you are going to Nurse, Mary Hanford."

The room got quiet, quieter than even Villa Hugel at night.

"What, *what* happened, Mary Hanford, to both of you? Bloody hell!" She shook me by the shoulder.

"I pushed her, Miss, didn't mean to hurt her. She fell on her back. Anne went through bushes to get her. It was all in fun, Miss. Couldn't snitch on Anne, now could I? Gentlemen don't snitch, do they, Miss?" Gordon's sharp falsetto reeked of contrition.

"You may return to your seats, ladies." Miss Sutton said as she stared across us at Gordon. "Would you come up to the desk and repeat that, Gordon?"

He came up to Miss Sutton and repeated with an embellishment that sounded lifted from a soccer game announcer.

"First, Mary, swanking about Americans—barbed my dad. Then I pushed, a sharp push. She fell—Anne in for the rescue. But I couldn't snitch, could I, Miss?"

Miss Sutton frowned and jerked out her elbows. "You are a disgrace to your class. Your father is an officer, is he not?"

"Yes, Miss."

"He will hear of this, you can be sure. Certainly, English gentlemen do *not* snitch. But, Gordon, more important, gentlemen *never, ever* push ladies. Do you understand?"

Gordon nodded.

"*What* do you understand, Gordon?"

"That English gentlemen never push ladies, ever." Gordon sighed

"What, Gordon, do you have to add?"

"That I am a disgrace."

"And?" Miss Sutton's lifted chin might have been searching the skies for enemy planes.

"Thank you, Miss."

"That's better. You may return to your place, Gordon." Miss Sutton watched while Gordon went back to his seat. Then just after he sat down. She turned sharply the way she did before giving an order.

"Class, open your books to Chapter Ten." Chairs scraped and papers crackled. "Now Benjamin Disraeli, the first Jew to serve as Prime Minister...." I didn't hear the rest because I went downstairs to see Nurse. Nurse wouldn't treat the wound until she got a shipment of peroxide, but I got better without it.

Afterwards, no one mentioned food, stones or Gordon's taking the blame. Nobody seemed so separate any more, not even me. We were more of one clump.

Chapter Nine

Argentina and the Absence of True Love

I had been playing Old Maid at the kitchen table because Emmy was baking again, this time, Volkormbrot, and I wanted to get a piece fresh out of the oven. Baking making always involved flour blizzards and hurricanes of Emmy's energy, and the flurry was always interesting. Emmy wasn't pretty but not ugly, I mean *ugly-ugly* either. Her brown hair tucked into a hairnet could be let down and brushed. She wasn't old and not fat. If she took off that faded green bib apron and put on a nice dress like Mommy's, she might show bosoms, if she had any. I think she did, because occasionally I saw bumps under her aprons. So why wasn't Emmy married and baking for her own children?

"Do you want children, Emmy?" I asked once.

"Yah, yah." She bent and turned on the oven.

"Then why aren't you married?"

"I was engaged once, before the war." She began wielding a huge, wood rolling pin, creating a flour cloud. Squish, squish went flour and butter as they glopped beneath the rolling pin

"Then why didn't you get married?" That seemed odd. Why wouldn't they get married immediately? That way, when fighting started, one could die in the other one's arms, the way they did in movies.

"He is in Argentina." She shrugged and then measured out some seeds.

"Argentina? South America?" I had studied geography in third grade, and Mommy had bought me a globe, but it hadn't gotten to Germany. So, I couldn't remember just where Argentina was, only that it was in South America which was connected by a tail to North America which held the United States. At that time, I wasn't even sure where Germany was, but knew Argentina was way far away from it. What did that have to do with anything? "So far away? You still could have gotten married. Or maybe you didn't want to move so far away?"

"It is very, very far away." Emmy actually sighed. I had never heard her sigh, only bark. "And he was an officer." She lowered her head a little.

"Oh, he was in the army?"

"It was the war. He had to go to Argentina." Crunch, crunch sounded the seeds as Emmy pounded the seeds with a pellet. And then threw them into the floury mixture which had yet to be kneaded. It was the darkest flour I had ever seen.

What did being an officer have to do with it? Or maybe German officers couldn't marry? No—that couldn't be true. Dr. Kort had been an officer and he was married. Emmy's was hiding something. I decided Emmy was hiding something because her answer didn't make sense and she was also speaking in the tone she used to tell me my parents wouldn't be back for a week. Maybe she didn't love her man. Maybe Emmy knew she was supposed to marry but didn't really want to.

"Emmy, do you love him, I mean really, really love him?"

Emmy scowled as if I had asked a hard math question. "He was a very nice man."

"But did you love him?" If she really loved him, she would have married him and gone to Argentina, if she was allowed. And why wouldn't she be allowed?

"He was a very, very nice man."

"What do you mean was? Aren't you going to see him again?"

She shook her head and then said, as if talking to herself, "But he had to go to Argentina." The wood was crackling so loud in the stove, I could barely hear her.

Argentina was probably an excuse not to marry him. "You're not telling me everything or you're leaving out something important. But it's all right. You can tell me."

But of course, she couldn't. I found out later, much later as an adult, that Nazi officers routinely escaped to pro-Nazi Argentina to avoid capture and/or to escape prosecution for war crimes. Only when I was close to middle age did I learn that Catholic Nazis had the edge in escape, that the church was complicit in getting them out of Germany. Even had Emmy a mind to correct my notions, she would have probably thought it beyond the ken of a child. And she would have been right. There was a conspiracy of silence about almost everything about the war. I didn't find out about the Final Solution until I was in college, although I picked up that Germans had done something terrible to Jews. When I asked Irmgard's family why the Nazis had done really bad things, "Ah, das Juden," Irmard's father had almost shouted, and said that they didn't know what was happening.

Suddenly Emmy dropped her fake sweet voice and stared at me with her hawk's eye. She swept dough into loaf pans. "It was *Argentina*," she said, her mouth a beak, ready to bite.

She slid the loaves into the oven. When the Volkornbrot came out, they were a shoe-brown color with a cracked crust that reminded me of parched earth. Emmy turned out the loaves and sliced them, even while they were hot, and they didn't stick. "Eat." She put two slices onto a plate. They were delicious; I reached for more. Emmy didn't stop me. Instead she put butter on the table. But I still wondered about Argentina and love. Emmy never answered me, but—then—stuffed with hot bread, I decided grown-ups were just like that, at least in Germany where leftover problems from the war were just like leftover bread crusts. It didn't matter to me, as long as I could eat the middles of whatever Germans baked.

Now I wonder about Emmy's lost marriage. She must have been devastated to see him and her dreams go. How much did she mark the irony of having to turn from keeping house for a husband and children, to keeping house for conquerors? Did she recognize that I profited from the children she was denied? Or was she simply glad she was alive with parts intact, not a POW or awaiting trial in Nuremburg? I'll never know; nor will she ever know how much her indelible warmth nourished my spindly spirit.

Chapter Ten

Villa Hugel and the Fine Arts

Sitting on the wood, spirally stairs in the Villa Hugel Great Room, waiting for Daddy, I saw that those chandeliers had lights stuck on small plates stuck on curved things which branched out. Yet they were all in a circle, one tier on top of another like a wedding cake, but then the buildings were that way also. And those lights lit up even the dark places in this huge place. They reminded me of what grown-ups said school was supposed to be, a place to En-Lighten your mind. Come to think of it, Villa Hugel was a school, just as much as that British school. That British place taught me history, literature and to "carry on." Villa Hugel taught that parties are just work, music can be as good as history and literature, swimming can help through tough times, and what seems true sometimes just isn't.

For example, in Villa Hugel those portraits of kids and horses in this hall are not true, although they are supposed to be. No one looks like that when actually on a horse, especially kids. I learned that much from my few riding lessons, and I wouldn't have had those lessons had it not been for one of the Villa Hugel British wives.

The Villa Hugel pictures of grown-ups are well done but also don't seem real. They aren't worth mentioning because they are boring.

Daddy worked up on another floor from the Great Room. I only went up there a few times. Anyhow, except for Anna, the secretary, no one paid any attention to me. If I had to wait for Daddy, I tried to wait downstairs somewhere, but sometimes I had to go to his office.

One time I was waiting in the Great Room, when I heard a woman singing. It was not coming from Daddy's place but somewhere upstairs. And there was lots of music for the woman singing. I waited, even though I could see the Mercedes waiting outside for Emmy and me, but Emmy was talking to someone so it didn't matter. I figured out that the high woman's voice and all the music was coming from a radio.

"Where's the radio? And who is that?" I said when Emmy finally came to get me.

"It's the BBC. Mind those steps. Come." Emmy hurried me through the door.

The next time I heard that radio, I was with Daddy, but it wasn't so awful, as there were only two or three people there. "That music, what kind is it, Daddy?"

"Oh, that. That music is from the Gibbs' radio. He likes opera." Gibbs was a Villa Hugel military man with a thin mustache. He had a daughter named Judy who had red hair and buck teeth and liked to play "Clue."

"What's opera?" I asked.

"That's music," Daddy said, looking for his briefcase, which was behind a big trash basket.

"Opera, *Machen,* is a play in which the actors sing instead of talk." Anna, seemed to know everything, from where to find a file to where to buy good sausage. She helped everybody at Villa Hugel, so people liked her even though she was German. Even though Anna was pretty, no one teased her as they did other German women. Maybe they didn't because she had just been married and was going to have a baby. I was glad because some teasing wasn't funny but dirty, or almost.

"A play with music in it?" I hadn't seen a play since second and third grades, and then they were Christmas plays which are always boring. Maybe this was a chance to do something other than swim and watch Friday night films. "Can I go, can I go?"

"We'll see." Daddy spotted his briefcase and picked it up. Then he got out a cigarette and lighted it. One thing good about the PX was that the cigarettes were cheaper.

"Frank, you ought to take your daughter to the opera in Essen. They still have quite a fine show, you know." Colonel Gibbs' thin mustache twitched. He lifted his chin up, as if proud or wanting to fight. "I heard from your wife that Mary Hanford is musical."

I remembered the two silver dollars I won in Richmond for playing "*The Three Trolls*" on the piano. Mommy wouldn't let me spend them and kept them in her jewelry box, where she occasionally got them out and told friends about them. Still, it was true I loved music, but I'm not sure that made me anything special; still I felt sad because I couldn't have piano lessons.

"Uh, huh," Daddy said. "Come on Mary Hanford; time, past time to go."

Daddy didn't take me to the opera, but at least I found out about what it was and that from Anna, a German. I also realized that my sadness was not only because I couldn't have piano lessons, but because I just plain missed music.

So, instead of opera I got involved with ballet. In Atlanta, I'd seen a movie of the "*Nutcracker Suite*" and marveled at the beautiful dancers. Young Mrs. Glass, who lived in Heisingen, had been a dancer once. Katie told me Mrs. Glass was giving ballet lessons to get her shape back after having her baby. She and Lucinda were taking lessons, so I went with Katie once or twice just to watch. Then Mrs. Glass encouraged me to join in, so I did. We stretched and curved our arms out in different positions and put legs, one after the other, on a railing stuck to a mirrored wall. We also had to bend our necks and heads just so. Mrs. Glass said we couldn't do "point," dance on our toes, until we got the positions right.

When we got positions wrong, which was almost always, instead of correcting or scolding us, she would show us the right way, flinging her leg upon the rail as if it were nothing and bending her thin body over so far that her beautiful black hair, usually worn up untwisted and flowed to her waist. When she showed us pictures of her dancing *Swan Lake* in white tulle and pink toe shoes, I yearned to be like her. Maybe if I stretched enough and danced around on my toes enough, I'd get thin.

So I told Mommy that I'd been going with Katy to Mrs. Glass's house and that now I wanted to take proper ballet lessons instead of just tagging along.

"The Glass house? Mercy, how did you get there?"

"I walked, first to Katy's house, and then we walked to Mrs. Glass' house."

"That must be almost two miles. Weren't you exhausted? I'm surprised you're not sick." Mommy frowned slightly, as if she had heard something she didn't quite believe.

"No, I feel better, not worse, especially after a lesson. Lessons would be good for me, would keep me in touch with music, so I don't forget everything. Didn't Miss Coles tell me to keep up with my music?"

She nodded.

Also, I told her ballet lessons would be no trouble because (a) Mrs. Glass was American, so she wouldn't have to find a German; (b) I could walk to Mrs. Glass' house. (c) Since I couldn't take piano lessons in Germany, ballet was the next best thing.

"And after all those lessons, which must have cost a lot, it would be a shame to forget, but if I don't have some kind of music, I will, won't I?" I hoped mentioning money would close the deal.

"I don't know about that. What does appeal to me is that you would be with friends, children of Americans I and your father know, not just playing with Germans you meet on the street." Mommy pulled out a Chesterfield from the pack and tapped it on an end table. She always did that when considering.

"All right, Darling, good idea. I'll tell your father about it the next time he phones." She put the cigarette back in the pack, got up from her chair and kissed me.

All day I daydreamed about dancing in pink toe shoes and a pink net skirt, the prima ballerina in *Giselle.* I'd only heard of that ballet, never seen it, but *"Giselle"* sounded so nice that I knew it must be lovely. If I couldn't have fairy rings, maybe I could learn to be a fairy, or almost—like those in that Shakespeare play where in summer, humans acted like idiots and fairies tried to save them.

A few days later, Daddy called and I heard Mommy talking about menus for dinner parties, liquor, Herr Prusnat's salary, the coal commission and ballet lessons. I assumed everything was arranged. But it wasn't. Mommy told me that Daddy "absolutely forbade" ballet lessons.

"Why?" It felt like a glass shattering, only the glass was me.

"Daddy told me that when he lived in New York, he lived there sixteen years you know, he dated a ballerina in the New York Ballet Company. After a performance, when he went backstage to see her, he would wait while she unwrapped her ankle ribbons and took off her toe shoes. When she did, he saw her feet were a bloody pulp, not once or twice, but every time. Yet, she wouldn't quit dancing, seemed obsessed with it. Daddy was sure she became permanently hobbled. No, he couldn't allow this to happen to his daughter. No, you couldn't take ballet lessons; no."

I couldn't believe my ears. Just as I was about to have some fun. "Oh, please, please—Mrs. Glass won't make my feet bloody. She's easy and careful. I promise!"

"Your father hardly ever says 'no' to you, Darling. This time, he's just looking out for your best interests."

"He hardly ever says anything to me, yes or no. Why pretend that he really cares about this? He's just doing this to be mean!"

Mommy puffed out her chest like Miss Sutton. "That's enough, Mary Hanford."

I hated her.

When Daddy came home the next night, I stayed in my room and wouldn't greet him. But no one came up to get me or even seemed to notice I wasn't there. Lying on my bed, I thought about Dieter, Irmgard, now me—how children were trapped by their parents. Then I returned to my heroines, Nancy Drew and Wonder Woman. Nancy would want to find out the cause of this injustice. Wonder Woman would act. Yes, she would grab her golden lasso and fly to the scene of the crime and confront the evildoers. So would I.

I jumped up and ran downstairs into where my parents were having refreshments and stood in front of Daddy with my elbows jerked out, like Miss Sutton.

"First, I couldn't continue my piano lessons, even though Mrs. Coles said I should. Then there was no more opera, even though Mr. Gibbs said you should take me, and everyone knows I am musical. Now you say no ballet which I want more than anything! What does an old ballerina in New York have to do with me? You just don't want to be bothered, that's all!" Solid in righteousness, I stamped my foot.

"Mary Hanford!" Mommy said.

"No, it's true. He doesn't want to be bothered or is afraid his British coal people will think he's swanking—or he's afraid of Krupp since he's out of jail or maybe he's afraid of McCloy, whoever that is, because he said McCloy lined his own pockets and protected a Barbie who murdered French people!" If I'd had a golden lasso I would have looped it over him and pulled hard, not to kill but to make him choke, make him suffer."

Daddy paled, then frowned as if he didn't understand a language. Then he stood up, wobbly, and started towards me.

"How dare you be so impertinent! What do you know about lining pockets?" I was going to say it was stupid for an amateur to try to line one's own pockets when a tailor could do it, but Mommy interrupted.

"Frank, please. She's just a child," I heard Mommy plead, as I ran out of the room, but then only murmurs as I slammed my bedroom door. I flung myself onto Raggedly Ann and sobbed. As usual, no one came to get me.

So that was that, until weeks later one night at dinner when we were all together. Emmy had cleared the soup (it came in little flowered cups with two handles, so it was okay to pick it up and drink), and we were quietly waiting for the entrée when Daddy broke the silence.

"I have looked into this opera matter, and it seems there really is quite good opera in Essen. The opera *Aida* is now playing. "Perhaps *Aida* might be a good beginning opera for Mary

Hanford," he said, and then he folded his fingers into a point and leaned back in his chair.

"*Aida?*" Mommy looked up; her eyes sparkled. "Oh, well—yes, it would be an excellent start for her—the pageantry."

"Of course, *we* couldn't take her. Not with this month's schedule." Daddy said.

"Certainly not."

Emmy came in with a platter of rouladen, my favorite dish short of sauerbraten. She started around the left of each of us to serve us, just as Mommy had taught her.

"But perhaps one of your friends could take Mary Hanford to see the performance," Daddy said. He nodded to Emmy who then served him some rouladen.

"Friends?" Mommy lifted her sparse eyebrows and widened her eyes.

"We'd make sure they had the best seats, front row or even a box, if available." He slipped his linen napkin from its ring, unfolded it and put it in his lap without looking down, but didn't start to eat.

Emmy put a rouladen on my plate. "Thank you." I hoped the rouladen had a huge pickle inside. "Thank you."

"You don't thank servants," Emmy hissed. I knew that but did it anyway. Emmy said I had to learn about social place, but I told her that in the U.S. no one had social places, that we were democratic, which meant all were equal. But now, I was beginning to wonder. If everybody was equal, why did Mommy teach Emmy how to serve? Why didn't Mommy serve on her own?

"Yes, perhaps this Mrs. Glass, if Mary Hanford is that fond of her."

"Mrs. Glass has a baby, Frank." Mommy picked at the cucumbers in vinegar, which were beside the dinner plate in a pink shell. Except for the lovely pink shell, cucumber sandwiches were better.

"Or Madame Dupuis, if she's back from Paris. Anna can probably find out." He picked his knife and fork and began cutting the roulade without looking at it.

"Oh, Frank." Mommy put down her salad fork.

"I know, I know. You two are hardly fans of each other."

"It's not that, Frank," Mommy stumbled.

"Frances, you know we are dealing with evidence of serious pilfering at Villa Hugel. We have no idea who took the wall hangings, silver and jewelry, but there is certainly evidence that someone or someones did. Now there is a claim for reimbursement, soak the Americans; petty revenge, if you ask me." He glowered towards the kitchen. "Where's the wine?"

"It's coming, Frank."

"The point is that I don't have time to deal with delicate social slights." He finally cut a piece of meat.

"What's pilfering?" I asked.

"Stealing, Honey," Mommy whispered.

My stomach twinged at the word "steal." When I was five, I had stolen two of Tiny Bits' yellow pencils and never confessed. But it didn't seem right to bring that up now, not when opera was in the offing. So I just listened to them.

In the end, Emmy took me to the opera.

Emmy and I had a seat at this theatre only two rows back. The theatre had balconies, but I was glad we were downstairs. I could see the music people down in a kind of ditch near the stage.

Emmy wore her hair down but gathered at the nape of her net into kind of a small snood, kind of nice, but the effect was not much different from the way she usually wore it in a bun high up on her head. The snood was green velvet and really pretty, but her old brown coat kind of spoiled everything because she didn't take it off until we were in the dark theatre so I didn't see what she wore underneath.

The curtains parted to a scene of singing people in warm weather clothes wearing lots of gold, real palm trees, fake buildings and crashing music. They sang not in German and not in English but something else, but I don't know what. From Emmy's quietness, I don't think she understood either. The play seemed to be about people in Egypt and a war which the singers had won. So, people were all happy and throwing flowers around. It was interesting but loud and long. So long that it got boring until a man came in riding an *elephant,* a real elephant! I'd only seen one, and that one was in a zoo. This elephant was so close to us that I forgot to get scared because I was so excited. The music when the elephant came in....was like thunder but wonderful, glorious thunder, but calmed down after the elephant came onto the stage. He stood there and slowly waved his trunk.

The main characters were a bronze girl in a ragged dress, another woman wearing purple and a small crown, and a tall fat man in nice, white clothes. After a while, I understood that the bronze girl and the big man kind of loved each other, and that the other woman didn't like it. I figured this was like Cinderella and the wicked stepmother. But the prince and the ragged girl ended up in a huge box in which they would die! That was a terrible way to end a love story, and I was almost sorry I had come to the opera. The music saved it.

The next morning I told Emmy, "I don't know why they had to spoil the opera at the end."

"Vat spoil?"

"They died."

"All die."

"Yes, but they didn't have to make it so happy before."

"Vat? Better to be sad before the end? Live life unhappy, then die?"

I knew she was trying to teach me but ignored her.

"I liked the elephant but not the play. Why should anyone pay to see unhappiness when anyone can see it in real life?"

Emmy paused and nodded.

"All last night, that thundering music that played when the elephant entered, even some of the other music, went round and round in my mind. Colonel Gibbs is smart just to listen to opera on the radio. It is too sad to watch!"

"Yah, it is. Poodle, now you get shoes on. Dress total." Emmy turned back to reading some kind of recipe in German.

***

But later, when I was in Villa Hugel and heard that kind of music, I wanted to find it. Usually, it was Colonel Gibbs' radio playing it, but sometimes I heard it coming from somewhere else in Villa Hugel. When Colonel Gibbs' radio was playing the opera, I would step behind his map and listen. Most of the time he just looked up and smiled, but once he told me that Germany had made operas before the war and that Germans had even written some. I asked Emmy if that was true that Germans have written operas as well as made famous composers. I knew Germans made my glimmering gingerbread house, and I knew the bakery that made it was smack in central Heisingen. Mommy had also bought the small child statues called Hummels and then blue cups and saucers called Meissen in Frankfurt. But those were small things; I hadn't put together that Germans could make something really grand, like opera with elephants and gold—no, grand and beautiful. After all, Villa Hugel was grand, but mainly ugly.

"Yah," she said.

"Then why did they start a big war?" It seemed to me that big and beautiful was opposite from war.

Emmy just shrugged and said maybe soon I would hear more opera music. But Colonel Gibbs got transferred and there was no more opera music, making Villa Hugel seem even larger and more empty.

Not everything at Villa Hugel was dreary. Its pool cushioned me from disappointments. As I said, it was a sanctuary. The boy sitting on the dark green fish had a jolly smile that cheered me. The green and white everywhere reminded me of spring flowers, no matter how cold it was outside. I could pretend I was in a deep pond during the summertime on a farm somewhere in Virginia, because I went to one once. When I was swimming in Villa Hugel's pool, it seemed like nothing bad had ever happened. I would do the breast stroke and close my eyes and then turn over and float. The sound of the water flowing from the fish was like water wind-chimes, and I could float far away like a gardenia carried downstream—only just as I was about to really let go, I'd bump against the pool's edge and have to wake up. Even though it wasn't a very big pool and had only a couple steps before deep water, it was okay. If I swallowed some water, it didn't even taste bad.

The best part was that it smelled like chlorine like the YMCA pool in Richmond, Virginia where we lived happily. I was glad Mommy had made me take swimming lessons at the YMCA there. Even though I was scared, I learned to put my head under water and then swim. Also, I loved the after-swimming hungry and the food in the YMCA cafeteria, except once when Mommy got a hot fudge sundae. I asked if ice cream was on her diet, and she got real mad and pushed the sundae away. I felt really bad that I had ruined her ice cream.

But at Villa Hugel, I didn't get after-swimming hungry. Instead I got cold. Still had to shower in the Kaiser's shower, which was freezing which is maybe why he got so mean. The Kaiser's shower was so big and tall, it had arches like in cathedrals, whose arches are held up by Flying Butts. The Kaiser must have been really tall, maybe even bigger than in the portrait in the Great Room. I felt like a dwarf in that shower and never seemed to get enough hot water to get warm or enough towels to get warm afterward. Once Emmy was late in picking me up, so I just got dressed and didn't shower. But she knew—I don't know how—and made me take off all my clothes and shower in the Kaiser's shower anyway.

The pool taught me that swimming could make you forget what was bothering you even if it was winter outside. You could dive down under those waters and be in Atlantis or in between layers like glass that kept you safe from stoning or being called names. The boy on the fish would laugh and say "Let's have fun— why are you thinking about school?" Sometimes when I was swimming under water, I would open my eyes and look through the layers and think I would see him put his horn to his mouth and blow it.

That boy helped me understand that people catch wrong notions that stick in their heads until someone blows a horn and blasts through lie-dust until you can see the truth at the bottom.

Even then, some won't swim to the bottom. I learned this at Villa Hugel's Friday night movies.

Emmy ended up being the one who took me to the Friday night films. Mommy had taken me at first, but later she was busy, and said to Emmy that if she would be so good as to take me, it would be all right with her.

The movies were always the same with good Americans and bad Germans, both in planes. At the end all the Germans would be dead and the starred American planes roared off in victory. The audience always clapped and congratulated each other after the show. People, especially soldiers, would laugh about Germans and make fun of them.

"Idiots thought they could rule the world."

"Dumb metal heads—all good for nothing except shoveling coal...."

"Yeah, in Hell," and everybody would laugh.

I began to worry about Emmy who sat ramrod straight through all this and never said a word. Hearing all this must be hard on her and it wasn't true anyway. I began to suspect those movies were bad for everybody.

One Friday night, as the lights came on, a freckle-faced, red-haired GI was chomping on Baby Ruths. He must have seen me earlier because he came over and offered me part of his second Baby Ruth.

"Here, Kid, have a bit of good ole American candy. Commissary got some in this morning. Sure beats..." He jerked his head towards Emmy. "...anything this kraut can give you."

I shook my head.

"Say, Kid, it cost tax-payer bucks to bring you decent candy." He gave a mock salute, indicating I should also. "Come on, Kid, don't look a gift horse in the mouth. It's a candy bar, not the Marshall Plan, which Krauts may be too proud, or stupid to take— or maybe we're the stupid ones for offering it, eh?" he said to the others.

I couldn't tell if he were talking about the candy bar or the Marshall Plan. "Yum, yum, Kid." He chewed loudly as if to convince me. The freckles on his face reminded me of pimples, pimples filled with pus. Something about those freckles and his caramel smeared teeth tipped me over the edge.

"No," I yelled and knocked the candy out of his hand.

"Hey, Kid." He backed off, eyes puzzled.

"You're not good, not super, not..." Emmy grabbed my arm, but I fought her off. "No, no! Leave me alone. You are my Emmy, mine. I love you, not them."

Everybody got quiet.

"Those movies are not all true, and if you think they are, you're 'metal heads' too," I yelled. Emmy grabbed my collar, like a cat lifts a kitten and pushed me towards the coat closet where our coats hung. Then she jerked out one of my arms and shoved a coat sleeve onto it.

"Whose brat is that?" Someone asked.

"I think Frank Baldy's daughter, but if so, she sure has grown," I heard Mrs. Forquin say.

"And if you think Germans are so bad, how come you let a German dog rescue Sondra?" I threw out to Mrs. Forquin.

"Mercy, it is his daughter. Poor Frank. Hardly a tribute to him," Mrs. Forquin said.

"Poor Frances, I should think," some woman added.

"Poor you," I yelled as Emmy forcibly buttoned my coat and pushed me at the stairs so hard I stumbled on the first three steps.

As Emmy dragged me out of Villa Hugel, her lips were a slit. She practically threw me into the Mercedes.

"I don't know why you're so mad, Emmy. I was just telling the truth." I rubbed my arm which was red from her grip.

"No one eats truth," Emmy snapped and refused to speak another word to me or the driver.

But I didn't care. I had blown my horn.

***

After my outburst nothing happened at first, except Mommy and Daddy had a discussion, not the usual rant, but a real back and forth talk. I knew it was about me, because they shut up when I came into the room. A couple days later, Mommy came to my room after dinner.

"Honey, I know you don't like just being in the house with nothing to do. School's out soon, and summer is very long. Would you be interested in going to a camp? An international camp in Switzerland?" She sat on the bed and stroked my hair. Then she showed me some pictures of the Jung Frau Mountain and Interlaken, which had a camp nearby.

"Sure," I said.

"Are you sure? It would be about a month. That's a long time to be away from home." She stroked my hair.

"Sure." I knew they were shipping me off. They probably wanted me out of the way, so they could smooth things over with the ex-pats. Suddenly, I felt sad and wanted….I didn't know what.

"Can I take Raggedy Ann with me?"

"I don't' see why not." She kissed me. Then I knew what I wanted—more hair strokes, another kiss. She ran her fingers through my hair.

"When do I go?" She ran her hand up and down my back.

"In a week. We've already sent in the application."

If my parents thought a month away would tone me down, they were wrong. Instead camp loosened what was choking me even more. No more dressing for dinner, etiquette, curtseying, Mommy's brushing my hair until it hurt, or having to protect Emmy. At the camp, I wore baggy pants, flunked housekeeping and didn't bathe or wash my hair for three weeks until the counselor made me. My roommates and I hung bloomers on our chandelier and one night we stole the cafeteria's cowbell—then put it back the next night. Each time I flunked deportment, I felt good. My nickname became "Duchess" after the curly-haired tomboy in the comic book "*Terry and the Pirates.*"

During our three-day hikes, I ate the black bread but refused the goat cheese, and no one hassled me. On the hikes we slept in obliging farmers' haystacks, flattening them by roughhousing. When a French counselor remarked that it was more natural for boys and girls to sleep together in the hay, a thrill coursed through me.

"Hey, Duchess," a tall boy called after that; his tone also thrilled, yet frightened me. It seemed safer to fall in love with our handsome Austrian counselor than to answer the boy. So I did. When I realized I could become a strong young woman like that snow-capped mountain, the Jung Frau, I uttered thanks to Villa Hugel's pool boy. If I hadn't seen him blow his horn, I wouldn't have blown mine.

Chapter Eleven

Frog Omen and Leprechauns

Things settled down at home and at school. I don't know if Villa Hugel's work changed, but Daddy did. He began to tell me bedtime stories, one about Umph and Whump, the mischievous hippos, and others about Percival the Pekinese. Percival would only eat rare filet mignon, and only if cut up properly. His owner, a very fat lady with frizzy yellow hair, carried Percival around on a big square silk pillow and never went anywhere without him, even to church. Daddy described Percival's curled plume tail and his yippity-yap so well that I always heard and saw him just before I drifted off. The only thing I didn't like was Daddy's description of Percival's owner, the fat woman. I was afraid Mommy's feelings would be hurt, as she was fat and never seemed to get thin, no matter how hard she tried. So far as I know she never learned about Percival's owner.

The Average table was working hard to complete school projects, which had been individually assigned. My project was to write on Ireland, specifically Irish history. I intended to write on the "Orange question," but instead a leprechaun story popped out. Once I got started on it, I couldn't stop. My leprechaun, Sean, was discouraged, because no matter how he tried, he couldn't find the pot of gold he was supposed to put at the end of a rainbow. Finally, he found out he was not really a leprechaun but an ordinary boy. His mother had thought him so special that she called him a leprechaun, even though he didn't have pointed ears. Relieved of his terrible burden, Sean decided to plant beans because his friend Jack did, and besides beans were kind of a gold in themselves. When a rainbow came, he just sat on the grass and admired it.

I drew a rainbow above the title and turned it in on the due date. But I worried. I had gotten carried away. My paper wasn't about the Orange question, and Miss Sutton was a stickler for directions. There was no time left to redo it.

I was stewing about this at home when Mommy startled me. "Would you like a birthday party, Dear? You'll be eleven in two weeks."

A party, a birthday party? For me?" I had one before when I turned six. Five people came. Sammy, my first boyfriend; Sara, his three-year-old sister; Lynn, daughter of Daddy's boss in Virginia; and Carol Helstein (She was Jewish but Mommy said it was okay because she was rich.) and Charlotte (Mommy didn't like her because her mother was a hairdresser and divorced but I insisted.). Mommy wrapped tiny gifts and put them on streamers in a bowl. We each picked one and tugged it out of the bowl. My prize was a tiny beer mug. There was also a cake with six candles and roses made out of icing. I wanted a rose, but Sammy did too, and we fought. I got it because I was the birthday girl but Sammy cut across the middle of it when Mommy wasn't looking.

So now when Mommy asked if I wanted a birthday party, I was so overwhelmed, I could hardly speak. So I didn't; I just nodded. After all, somehow I had made it through a year at "the British School." Although I still couldn't calculate British money, Dawn had stopped harassing me, and even Gordon and I spoke. Also, since the stoning incident, we didn't seem so separate, maybe because I didn't snitch. Still I didn't know if anyone would come to my party, but I didn't tell Mommy because she was excited to be planning another event.

The day I was going to pass out the invitations, Miss Sutton passed out our projects with grades on them. On my story, underneath the rainbow I'd drawn was an "Excellent" scrawled in Miss Sutton's jumping-bean handwriting. I was stunned; I have never made a "Good +"much less an "Excellent Minus." This was an Academic table grade.

"Ooooooo, Look at you! An American gets a good British grade. Extraordinary." Lucinda had been standing behind me, peeking.

Dawn snatched the paper from me and almost all the average table peered at it, commenting. Now again they wouldn't like me, would say I was "swanking," would say I cheated. I shoved the rubber-banded invitations under the table.

"You, back there at the center table. What are you jabbering about? "Go back to your places and carry on." Miss Sutton ordered. They scurried back but not until Lucinda glimpsed the stack of rubber-banded invitations under the table.

"What's that?"

"Nothing." I put my hands over them.

"Don't tell me you've got all 'Excellences' bound up there," she snickered. "And in tiny envelopes?"

"I don't; I don't. These are invitations. Quiet." I heard my voice tremble.

Trying to control my shaking, I unbound the invitations and passed them under the table, each student taking one and handing off the others.

After a muffled clatter of ripping envelopes, that Miss Sutton didn't notice, Gordon and Anne looked at me and nodded vigorously.

Dawn waved her invitation as if fanning herself. "Well, it's about time. We knew you had a birthday from Girl Guide forms. We hoped you'd have a party before anybody got transferred. I've told them about your house in Heisingen. You'll be the first of our set to have a proper birthday."

Our set? Our set? "You mean you'll come?" I didn't dare ask about other parties.

"Why wouldn't we?" Anne asked.

"You'd better check the RSVP box, Chaps," Gordon muttered and licked the inside envelope.

The long afternoon of June 18th spread golden rays until nearly nine at night. Promptly at four, Anne, Gordon, Dawn, Donald, Karen, Scott, Lucinda, and a few others showed up. We gathered in the dining room where Mommy piled presents on the table, beside a platter of cucumber and watercress sandwiches and gave out little pointed party hats. Irmgard came but stood apart from the others.

"Happy Birthday," she said and put a present on the grand piano.

Then we played Blind Man's Bluff outside. When I took off my blindfold, Irmgard had disappeared.

Emmy brought out a German chocolate birthday cake, orange squash and vanilla ice cream from the commissary.

Everybody sang "Happy Birthday" as I blew out the candles. These people who had teased me, shut me out, even thrown stones at me, *sang* to me. I couldn't make a wish because I already had everything I wanted. Warmth spread through me like the warmth on my legs when I wet my pants. But this warmth wasn't from an accident and it expanded through all of me like candles' glow grow outward.

Gordon shoved a tiny present at me. "Real silver," he said, looking at the floor. Inside the packaging was an oval pin rimmed in silver, a portrait of trees and flowers painted on the brightest blue background I ever saw. Anne helped me put it on.

"How come it's so blue?" I asked.

"Oh, it's painted on butterfly wing. But it's *real* silver," Gordon said.

"Wow, butterfly's wing." That was far more exciting than silver.

"Good, eh?" Gordon again examined his feet. He was red in the face.

"Oh, thank you!" I hugged him, but he pulled away with an "Ugh" and began running. "Can't catch me." I took off after him. Pretty soon we are all running, Emmy guiding us into the lawn

"Catch me if you can," Donald yelled.

We raced around, hiding behind bushes, trees, grabbing and scaring those who ran past, breaking into twos, then threes, then groups, exuberant in the emerald grass and golden light laced with honeysuckle fragrance. At six when parents or servants arrived to pick up the guests, they gushed to my mother, "What a nice child, beautiful place."

All for me—a party, a successful party—at last. How had it happened? Despite curly hair, being fat, a "rich American" and hopeless at British money, I, now eleven, had friends and an "Excellent Minus" on my paper. With a baffled giddiness I climbed into bed. As my head hit the pillow, tobogganing boys, kids colliding on a summer's evening, and Irmgard's crocheted present danced in my head. I didn't need to talk to Raggedy Ann or wait for the Indian to tuck me in.

"Real silver," chuckled Emmy the next morning, as she cleared the breakfast dishes and the remnants of the birthday bash.

"That boy, he likes you."

"Who, Gordon?"

"Yah."

"Like, like 'love'?" I felt goose bumps rise.

"Poodle, you—too young for love."

A boy liked me? Liked me like...? The possibility, plus the party and the Excellent Minus addled me. I felt as if I had gone to heaven and Seven Elasse Str. was one of its "many mansions" especially compared to the house in Decatur where we only lived in half of it.

Certainly, the house's interior was striking, thanks to Emmy, but it was the outside that was ambrosial. Herr Prusnat had littered the lawn with roses, daffodils, trillium and violets. Honeysuckle twined around tree trunks and trellises. With Joey gamboling by his side Herr Prusnat planted, pruned, transplanted and weeded until the grounds rioted with color and fragrance. He destroyed a pool of algae, floated white water lilies on it and fixed the center fountain, so it went off at night right after sunset. Then there would still be colors in the sky and the fountain spray would twinkle with rose and gold.

Wrapped in the cocoon of success, I began to stroll around the lawn and pool in the evenings, not only to see the fountain spurt in Technicolor but to bask in iris-colored shadows and the quiet between the clack of Emmy's shutting blinds and the chimes of the village clock. Like the woods beyond, Seven Elasse Str. was so full of something, something I couldn't see, and I was its princess or maybe wood or water sprite.

One night I stayed out after nine. Mommy and Daddy weren't home, and Emmy didn't care. It was black night and a chill had crept through the evening hush. I was ambling past the pool when "Thrump, rump" thundered from it. I stood, helpless with fear. *An angry river god? No—a pool isn't a river.* Silence, only this time the quiet seemed ominous. Then just as I began again towards the house, "Thrump, stumfp!" echoed from a hollow place, and shrieking, I fled into the house.

"Emmy, Emmy." I raced three-at-a-time upstairs to the servants' quarters. "Out there, out there...." I pointed toward the back yard.

"What, Poodle, What?" Emmy stood up ramrod straight. "Stay. You not breathe."

"Out there." I buried my face in her skirts. Emmy threw on a coat, grabbed my hand and we hurdled downstairs out into the yard.

"Du poodle—stay." Emmy pointed for me to stay near the backyard door. Then she strode the perimeter of the grounds jerking her head in all directions with the regularity of a metronome. Nothing. Only the sounds of crickets and a few things rustling somewhere.

Emmy came back to me and put her hand on my shoulder. "For this, you bring me out?"

Then suddenly, "Thrump, stumfp, rrrrrr...." I jumped and clutched Emmy. "That, that—you hear, you hear?"

Emmy laughed, low and guttural, and then pulled me towards the pool. I resisted but her arm was strong and I was too scared to yell. "Look." We stopped at the pool's edge. "Open eyes," Emmy commanded. How had she known I had shut them?

I opened them to no light, except that upstairs on the third floor. Emmy took her two hands then put each one on the side of my head, forcing it to look in a certain direction. But all I saw was fog, or thickness—until a mound the size of a big rock began to shape itself as my eyes accustomed themselves to the dark. The mound was blotched or spotted. "Thrumph!"

"Frog," Emmy said. I squinted and through narrowed eyes made out two mounds, a head and a body. Yes, frog, just frog. Only frog.

***

"But why was it so loud?" I asked as Emmy stacked pillows on the kitchen chair so I could reach the hot chocolate she'd mysteriously decided to make.

"Because it is omen. Now sit," Emmy said.

"What's that?

"Means change." She smacked clean cups and saucers into the cabinet.

"Omen means change? Good or bad change?"

Emmy didn't answer, but plunked down steaming cocoa on the kitchen table.

"Omen is sign that things will change." I settled into sipping the hot chocolate

"Yah," Emmy nodded.

"But you haven't told me good or bad change."

"Just change." She ran her finger across a window sash searching for dust and something in a corner skittered. A mouse. A roach?

"Well, should I be afraid?"

Emmy bored her falcon eyes into me. "It is never good to be afraid. As she swooped down to get my cup, she tousled my hair with a vigor that said "face things."

"Now, sleep."

I went to bed, strangely comforted.

Chapter Twelve

Krystal Clear

Boys and girls often played in the street beyond the imposing iron gate of my house. They often played with a toy which consisted of a wooden painted cup, or "bowl" shape with a handle under the base and a ball on a string attached to the bowl. You'd throw the ball up and then try to catch it in the bowl. One of them, Krystal, was eleven, had long blonde braids and spoke English. Krystal showed me how to use the toy and got mad when the boys laughed at me.

One day I went home with Krystal for lunch. Her house was wood and small with lots of people whom I took to be German; at least they spoke German. There was Krystal's mother, a man about her age, whom I took to be Krystal's dad, several old people, two women and one man, and also young men and women. Krystal had two brothers and one sister. I had met Krystal's mother, a large washed-out looking woman who always wore a complete, usually faded, apron. Her hair was tucked into an impromptu bun, and I couldn't decide if it was blonde or grey. The dad sat away from the others at a small table writing something. The old people sat in three wood chairs, two of them wobbly, at a huge oblong kitchen table. The old man was very short and had his head on his chest, sleeping. One elderly woman sat ramrod straight, peeling potatoes. She was dark, and raisiny and never said a word. On the other hand, Krystal's grandmother, who was spaetzle dumpy with thin grey hair pulled back into a bun so tight I could see her skull, chattered all the time, punctuating with whatever she was saying with lightning quick gestures. Krystal's mom looked like her, only stretched on a larger frame and with more hair. Of the younger men and women, one guy was ultra-short but had really strong-looking arms; he had been a printer before the war and had to lift heavy printing plates. The other man was tall and skinny blond with rabbity eyes and looked as if he didn't have eyebrows, but he did. You just had to look closely.

Two women had braids like Krystal, only one blonde and the other brown. Constantly one set the table; another chopped cabbage, both snapped orders to each other. Another woman, with dark hair and pale skin stayed near the stove. She was pretty and slim, except for a poochy stomach and reminded me of a tired Snow White. But she just sat near the stove, not doing or saying hardly anything. The kitchen was so crowded; the whole house was small, so how could everyone fit? Where would they sleep?

The house hadn't been bombed but the front steps and porch had broken places in them, so you had to watch where you stepped. The back steps were gone; you could tell by the drop from the kitchen back door that once steps had been there. Buckets dotted the living room, so I guess the roof leaked. Nails stuck up at odd places in the kitchen and so did boards. Colored pictures of Jesus and people Krystal called "saints" hung in the tiny living room, making the place feel even more crowded. Those painted people peering down gave me the creeps, as if they were asking questions I didn't know how to answer.

It seemed odd that I lived with Mommy and Daddy in such a huge house, and Krystal lived in this tiny place with fifteen people at least. I didn't know if Germans had always lived this way or whether after the war they could not afford better. Irmgard's house was tiny but not broken down; also only four people lived there. And Irmgard's family had a vegetable garden in back, which seemed to be a big deal.

"This tiny ground saved us during the war," Irmgard's mother said over and over again, but she never said why. Maybe Germans just lived in little places. But what about Villa Hugel? It was grand—a palace. The allies worked there, so maybe they had fixed it up. But underneath I knew this wasn't true—that there had been some very rich Germans, Krupp anyway, and those people who once owned the big houses where now the allies lived. So where were they? They couldn't all be in basements.

Except for the old man asleep and the sad-looking woman on the stool, everybody was working, working. Yet all I did in my huge Heisingen house was read books, dodge Calvert Course lessons and hang around Emmy. It was as if I were eating apple strudel and my friends had only dark, stale bread, no matter how hard they worked. But strudel doesn't taste as good, if only one is eating. One can share dessert, but I didn't think my house could be easily shared, particularly after the way Irmgard acted when I wanted her to swim with me in Villa Hugel's pool.

Not everyone stayed in Krystal's house, because only eight sat down to eat mashed potatoes and red cabbage. The cabbage tasted wonderful, like Emmy's sauerbraten red cabbage. Krystal mixed the cabbage with the potatoes, purple swirls through ivory. When she did it fast, they reminded me of pictures I'd seen of whirling dervishes in National Geographic. So I swirled mine too, and it tasted even better. I waited for the meat but there turned out not to be any.

One of the old men said grace I think. Then everyone had helped themselves and began to talk. I couldn't speak German, but could understand some. When I heard "American….something about a girl and child" the old men stiffened and the printer guy looked down. The Raisin woman waved her arms and her voice rose, screechy like someone calling for help. Then she got up and went into another room. Then everybody started interrupting each other. Krystal's grandmother scrunched her face, and wiped off a tear with her apron, finally, the woman with the brown braids shoved her chair back from the table, got up and brought a big bowl of ginger cookies to the table. She was glad the Raisin woman was gone. Krystal's mom served coffee, and everybody got okay with drinking coffee and eating cookies. I stayed very quiet but knew something had happened involving Americans; maybe they had rescued some old people, and the Raisin woman was jealous. Maybe Americans had gotten some Germans better houses.

Later, when the kitchen was cleared and cleaned, Krystal and I sat on what was left of the porch. She was drawing something in the dirt with her shoe heel, when I asked, "I heard your family talking about an American, maybe a child—someone who couldn't go home?"

Krystal drew her foot back quickly and looked at me hard. "You speak German?" she sounded as if it were a crime.

"No. I just understand some."

Krystal pulled back her braids and tied them at the back of her head as she sat straight up. "Well, an American soldier forced my cousin."

"Huh?" Why was Krystal jutting out her chin?

Krystal shifted on the broken porch step and looked down, as the printer man had done at dinner. Her face drooped. "You know—forced my cousin to do *it*. Now she has a baby."

"Forced to do *it*?" I felt myself go cold. *It* was something I didn't want to talk about or believe it was really true. In Atlanta, when Mommy had explained about babies, I cried because it was so gross. Since then, I'd managed to put the horrible thing out of my mind.

Krystal nodded. "Now her village won't accept her." She began digging in the dirt again.

"Was it that dark, pretty woman who didn't eat with us?"

Krystal nodded. "She was only here for the day; she has to get a job."

Forced. An American. I just couldn't wrap my mind around it. "But it wasn't her fault. It wasn't your cousin's fault. Did they throw her out because the man was American?"

"Yes *and* he was black." Krystal sighed. "Now she has a black American baby." Krystal let a big sigh, and now I knew why.

It was impossible. Blacks served coffee and cleaned house. They took care of yards and babysat. Mommy said they stole and stank, but I never believed that. From what I gathered, black people needed white people for direction, organization and to bail them out of jail when they were drunk. It wasn't their fault. Just as I wasn't good at math, blacks weren't as good as whites in some things. White people had to stay white in order to direct things. "Purity," Aunt Page called it.

In Germany, in the PX and in the commissary, it was the same, blacks helping whites. "Boy, get me a carton of cigarettes." "Gal, clean off this table." (even if the black woman was an old woman) The Germans I knew referred to the "Swartzen" and laughed, but not a good laugh, when they saw black soldiers.

"What's going to happen to the baby? Is it a boy or a girl?"

"Girl." Krystal shrugged

A girl was worse somehow, although I wasn't sure why. "That man must be waiting for a court martial." I didn't really know what a "court marshal" was, except that it was terrible.

"He is in America." Krystal's face hardened, and she got up. "Now I have to clean the kitchen."

"It's already cleaned," I said. Without answering or even looking at me, Krystal went inside.

I started walking home. There was some mistake, or Krystal was lying. The radio at home, the newsreels, the films at Villa Hugel, the "Marshall Plan," whatever that was—showed Americans as superheroes. Americans rescued people. They risked their lives, even died for them. Americans didn't force—especially women, especially *it*.

I looked up to gauge the change in the rain. As I did, I glimpsed one side of a peaked-roofed, bombed-out building with a crumbled, brick chimney. One side was completely gone, like the open side of a doll house, but the rest was partially intact, its rubble still piled on the side. Apparently it once had three floors. On the third floor stuck a bit of blackened bedroom floral wallpaper; on a floor below a ceiling light still dangled by a flimsy wire. These scraps reminded me of burned-up Halloween decorations. One of the first I saw when we moved here was the half-steeple of a damaged church in the town center. Why hadn't I noticed these buildings so much closer to me? Why weren't these buildings fixed or razed like the others? I'd asked Daddy once why some building were not yet fixed, and he said the Marshall Plan had to do things slowly, one step at a time.

Maybe it was because I was upset about Krystal's cousin, but, for the first time, I realized that we, the Americans with the stars on our planes, had killed the people who lived in those bedrooms, who read under that ceiling light, who worshipped in that church. *We* had killed the very people who now took care of me! My stomach cramped, and again I tasted lunch's cabbage. Why had this not soaked in before? The irresolvability of it sickened me. This wasn't like a math problem, where if you worked the steps right, there was an answer, whether it was in dollars, shillings or marks. [No, everything about right and wrong was all mixed up, no matter what was said in movies, in the *"Stars and Stripes."*] I moved from the road to the grass, bent over and vomited. Irmgard, the faces of Emmy, Krystal, Hannahlore, Manfried, and Herr Prusnat flashed through my mind as I retched. Americans killed them, or people like them. Americans forced *"It"* on girls, got them thrown out of their homes, made old ladies move into their own basements.

I'd been lied to—worse—everyone had been lied to. Or was it that everyone lied? Maybe this terrible truth was worse than the lies. No—it couldn't be—those lies made people do horrible things. I retched and retched, as if I could vomit out the invisible poison that polluted everyone—like gas. Only no one had gas masks; we were *all* poisoned: Emmy and Herr Prusnat and Irmgard, Mommy and Daddy, Mrs. Glass and Karen—only Americans pretended *not* to be.

Nothing more came out, and my stomach ached from heaving. I flung myself onto the ground in the drizzle, exhausted from wrestling with the truth, fighting the knowledge that refused to be held back.

The drizzle started to morph into big drops like tears. I thought about going back to Krystal's to borrow an umbrella, but instead I sloshed through puddles. The rain felt like getting clean after a shower, although I don't know why I felt dirty.

As I sloshed, I pondered everything. Americans not being superheroes or blacks and whites doing *it* had never entered my mind. But even worse than that was the *forcing.* Krystal must be lying, but why? After all, I had asked the questions. My stomach churned and cramped, in, out, in, out. I wanted to throw up again, so stood by a tree and retched. It tried to come up—you know, "Uhhh, Uhhh, Uhhh," but no stuff came out. Finally the storm inside me quieted but I still felt dull and gray, and I ached. I told myself that the ache happened because no potatoes or cabbage had come up, but sensed that the really bad stuff would never come up. Nothing was altogether good. Just like babies came from something gross; just like steaks meant killing an animal; Americans winning could be bad. The song *Blue skies, nothing but blue skies, nothing but blue skies from now on*" ran through my head, as if mocking me. It was the song that lied, not Krystal. There weren't blue skies somewhere always—everything wouldn't always look better in the morning—things didn't always turn out for the best. And worse—nobody had warned me.

"You are sopping!" Emmy frowned as I pushed through the kitchen door. "And you've been crying. What happened?"

I stood dripping on the immaculate black-and-white tiled floor, smelling clove-studded pot roast on the stove and hearing the soft bubbling of dumpling water. Emmy moved deftly from one countertop to another. There were no nails sticking out of boards to impede her, and no kitchen table jammed up against cabinets. Beyond her were spacious rooms with wine-velvet furniture, large windows and gilt mirrors. My bedroom's built-in bed had feather quilts, which I never had to share, but now wished I could. Now those rooms beyond our kitchen loomed dark and empty, a huge mouth into which I could disappear. For an instant, I feared the house might eat me, and no one would find out. Only the kitchen, with its warmth hissing from the coal-driven boiler, the clashing smells of roast and baking apples and its militant commander seemed safe.

"Machen!" Emmy snapped, wiping her hands on her apron, and then grabbing a fresh wooden spoon. "Du poodle, answer me. Vas es los?" She shook her head. "You're dirty and wet, sash untied, caked with mud. Where have you been?"

"Nowhere."

"Nowhere?" She banged the air with the spoon.

"At Krystal's house." The tiles on the floor, if you looked at them with squinty eyes could seem diagonal.

"Krystal's!" Emmy's yellow hawk eyes burrowed into me, but they couldn't cover the concern in her voice. She strode over to me and placed her hand on my forehead. "Es du kranke?" The touch went through me like an electric message. It was strong and gentle, the way Gabral might feel if I could ride him, the way the breeze felt in Atlanta and the way Mommy's lap felt when I skinned my knees. "Nein," Emmy sighed, then stooped to face me eye level. "Vas es los?"

How could I tell Emmy that truth was not really true, that everything was a mess? I didn't have the words. Besides, I sensed she already knew. That was worse, or maybe better. What now staggered me and made me mute, was Emmy's hand. It told me that, despite the poison—*despite it*, Emmy loved me. I knew that deep down, but now it was on the surface. I had to let Emmy think I was still innocent, because if she knew I knew, then what would she do? Take sides, be forced to do *it?* That mustn't happen. I couldn't let her down.

"Nothing," I croaked "Nothing, just tired." I threw my arms around her and kissed her neck, because I couldn't reach her cheek. Then I ran upstairs. Clutching Raggedy Anne, I whispered to those beady eyes my revelation—that nothing was as I'd thought and that the main thing was to escape being swallowed into space and silence.

Chapter Thirteen

A Funnel into Sadness

Sometime after I got back from camp, Daddy started to travel to Frankfurt a lot more. He usually went to visit his American boss, Sid Wilner, who was stationed there. Sometimes Mommy and I went with him. The Wilners had a daughter, Karen, whom I really liked and who also liked me.

Sid Wilner was bald with a ring of dark hair like a monk which he wasn't because he was Jewish. He would stroll with his hands in his pockets as if he and Daddy weren't talking about anything important.

"Frank, much as I admire your intellect and integrity, I can't endorse what you want to do. Let us remember that foreign affairs are not a Sunday School picnic. More to the point, you are not in charge." Mr. Wilner had big brown, sad eyes that darted around. Those sad eyes made me like him because although he was quiet, he looked like he thought about things. He didn't wear a suit.

Karen's mom was from Arkansas and Daddy said "too smart for an Arkie." She was taller than Sid Wilner, with the large square face and set expression of one with definite opinions. Her eyes were squinty and her soft brown hair hung in a wispy shoulder-length pageboy. She believed in the New Deal, and Montessori Schools; she didn't believe in capital punishment, which meant killing people who murdered someone, so I don't know how she justified the war. She also didn't believe in inherited wealth, which meant that when parents died they left their money to their kids. But what else would dead parents do with their money? Mrs. Wilner was very smart and must have been a chemist for she understood labels. Once at the commissary, Karen wanted a bottle of Johnson's *Baby Magic* because it smelled so good. Mrs. Wilner turned the bottle over to read the label. "Mineral—that's all right."

Her eyes got extra squinty. "Laurel Sulfate" *and* "artificial fragrance."

"No, Karen. Absolutely not," Mrs. Wilner snapped. Without any discussion she put it back on the shelf

Once, to keep "American culture alive abroad" the Wilners invited us for Thanksgiving Dinner in Frankfurt. Mr. Wilner answered the door in pants like Herr Prusnat might have worn and a checked, open-necked shirt. Daddy was in a suit as he always was, and Mommy had on a French, blue silk dress. They made me wear a pleated Black Watch jumper and white blouse. Karen was in brown corduroy pants and tan pullover that almost matched her hair.

There were no decorations of Pilgrims or anywhere, but there was a pumpkin in the center, and plates and bowls set out on a blue print tablecloth. It was so unlike the linen, fine china and sterling silver tablescapes that Mother had at holidays that first I thought I was at breakfast on a kitchen table.

Mrs. Wilner came out of the kitchen wiping her hands on a big dish towel. She wore a very long brown blouse over a brown skirt which reached to her ankles with two feathers stuck behind her left ear. One feather was long and brown speckled; the other short and bright blue. Mother and daughter look-a-likes, I decided, although Karen didn't have feathers or her mother's calm, the kind of calm that gave me the willies. Karen was just quiet.

But Karen's mom was queenly, as she sat and said a Thanksgiving prayer. That prayer was to the Great Spirit, nothing like the "not worthy to gather up the crumbs under your table," stuff the British school had taught. Mrs. Wilner said usually Thanksgiving ignored the Indians when they were the first to bring corn to the first feast. And we had stolen their land. Then she got up and went back into the kitchen while we nibbled Commissary potato chips and waited for the turkey. Mrs. Wilner brought out bowls of sweet potatoes, white potatoes, spinach, kale, parsnips, carrots and a platter of something covered by a dishcloth. But no turkey. No one said anything until she brought the rolls, and it was obvious that there was going to be no turkey.

"You must be a vegetarian. These parsnips are delicious." Mommy twitched a little as she talked to Karen's mom who nodded. That was a lie because Mommy didn't like parsnips. Besides she always twitched when she lied.

"Frances studied the culinary arts at the Cordon Blu," Daddy said, reaching for the napkin ring, then glancing to find only an unringed cotton napkin.

"Cordon Blah!" Sid Wilner laughed. "These rolls are great! Are you sure you didn't baste them with butter, some poor creature's fat?"

"Oh, please!" Mrs. Wilner shook her head.

"Well, if not fat, how about some 'essential organs'?" He pointed to a platter that had a dish towel cover over it. "She may be vegetarian but she knows how to eat your heart out." He laughed louder than I'd ever heard him.

"Ugh, Daddy," Karen said. He took off the dish towel and handed her the platter on which lay what looked like a big heart, but was really liver.

"You were very brave to make all this on your own," Mommy said, helping herself to a liver slice and pushing some parsnips under kale.

"Well, pregnancy is not a disease, and I don't approve of servants, especially exploiting Germans in that manner. Haven't they been humiliated enough?"

Without even noticing Mommy's red face, Mrs. Wilner launched into telling us the progress of her project to get the Allies to build an SPCA.

"Actually, Sid, I'm glad you mentioned 'creatures.' I've been getting quite a response from the general's wife and her friends about the allies raising money for a Frankfurt SPCA. All those desperate animals wander about the rubble—it's enough to…" she dabbed at her eyes with her napkin.

"Want some more red meat, Frank?" Sid Wilner broke in.

Daddy stayed quiet except he asked for another glass of water. The Wilners didn't drink alcohol or even milk.

"Want some more red meat, Frank?" Sid's voice was jocular. "Red meat, Red, get it? He passed Daddy the liver which he had made into thick slices. "Thought you'd want the Reds in pieces," he laughed.

"I'd prefer whole Americans to sliced Reds," Daddy said.

"Oh, yeah, well, not everyone is of your opinion."

The good thing about Mrs. Wilner's rant about the SPCA was that no one noticed I didn't eat any liver. Daddy and Mr. Wilner went from "Reds" to "state business," which seemed to take their minds far away.

"Sid, let us remember this is a holiday, not work. Don't you think you should include us, as well? And I mean the children, as well. They might have questions. Do you children?" Mrs. Wilner said "children" as if she were talking to ducks or first graders.

Karen didn't say anything, but I did. "Did you know your hair looks like monks' hair?" I asked Mr. Wilner

"Ho, ho, that's rich! Well, I probably got my baldness from working for the U.S. government or maybe from reading the Torah since I was younger than you."

"What's Torah?"

"It's scripture we read in services."

"You mean the Bible?" I was pretty sure it wasn't the *Book of Common Prayer,* or Melanie would have mentioned it.

"Actually yes, Old Testament, but it's a bit different from churches."

"How is it different? I've heard churches read that before." I knew this was not the kind of question Mrs. Wilner wanted, but I was curious. What was the difference between Christian and Jews? I knew something bad had happened to Jews during the war, so why didn't it happen to Christians since they used the same book? Maybe that book was dangerous.

"Yes, Old Testament— but it's a bit different from churches."

Instead of answering, Sid turned to Daddy. "Frank, although this is very pleasant, may I have a word with you?" As he and Daddy got up to go into another room, Sid put his arm on Daddy's shoulder which was hard to do because Daddy was taller. Even though he was trying to be jolly, he wasn't for he walked with his head down.

"MacArthur has lots of supporters, so does McCloy. You don't want to be thought..." They went into another room. Then Mommy offered to help with the dishes, and Mrs. Wilner said yes, so Karen and I went into her room.

I asked Karen why we didn't have turkey. Karen told me her mom thought killing animals was wrong.

"But there was liver," I said.

"Her doctor said she had to eat liver because she was pregnant. Most of the time, I don't miss meat, but I would like to read a comic book now and then, if just to know what's so exciting about them."

"What? Any comic book? You don't read comic books?"

Then Karen told me she wasn't allowed to read comic books at all. Not even the ones I was allowed, Donald Duck, Mickey Mouse, nothing violent, like Batman or Superman. Even Wonder Woman was iffy, but she usually just lassoed people. Karen said she had always wanted to read comics; she didn't care what kind, but she knew her parents meant it for her own good. Her mouth pursed when she said that. I could tell she wanted to be like other girls, just like I wanted to be British.

That Karen was not allowed to read comic books seemed grossly unfair. This injunction reminded me of Deiter's severity about cherries. Karen was smart and nice; she never said a bad thing or even looked at me crossways. She was also helpless. What kind of life would it be with no hamburgers, and no Donald Duck? So the next time we all went to Frankfurt, I took about thirty of my favorite comics and shoved them under the clothes in my overnight bag.

Karen's eyes opened really wide when I lifted my clothes and showed her what was beneath them. She smiled big, the first time I'd even seen her grin.

"Wait until tomorrow," Karen whispered. "That's when Mother has naps scheduled."

The next day at three o'clock, everybody was supposed to nap, except the men who were arguing about something.

"Frank, Abe Fortas told me you were conceptual, but I had no idea...." Sid Wilner said.

"I remember that. What do you suppose he meant, Sid?"

"Let's just go talk to the boss and try to settle something." So Daddy and Sid left for the I.G. Farben building even though Mrs. Wilner had scheduled naps. After they left, Mrs. Wilner and Mommy ordered us upstairs, and they went to the second floor themselves.

Wilners' Frankfurt house had three floors. Karen's room was on the third floor. After a while, we sneaked down to the second floor, where Mommy and Mrs. Wilner were napping, like we were supposed to be doing. As soon as we heard someone snoring, we tiptoed back upstairs to Karen's room.

Karen closed her door. and I got out the comic books and spread them on the twin bed I'd slept in—Donald Duck and Huey, Dewey and Louie, Mickey Mouse, Henry the Chicken Hawk, Doopy the Hound, even a whole comic book devoted to Scrooge McDuck. There were also a few Wonder Woman comics (a grey area but Mommy let me have them) and hordes of Comic Classics. "The Man in the Iron Mask," and "Silas Marner." Karen's face shone like Christmas lights. (The Wilners didn't do Christmas either.) She gathered a bunch and sat cross-legged with them on her bed. She picked up one, then another, and another comic as if they were jewels. Her olive skin glowed and her mouth turned up in a tiny smile, a Mona Lisa Comic Book Madonna. The sun streamed through the windows, so bright we didn't need lamps, and warmed our legs as we sprawled on the beds. To be warm, and cozily reading with a friend seemed another mansion in Heaven.

Karen had thrown the comics she had devoured into a loose pile at the foot of her bed, so that they threatened to fall off. When I heard a slight squish, I assumed it was the comics landing on the floor.

"Well, this *is* a surprise," Mrs. Wilner said. The squish source stood in the open doorway. Her voice held a hint of contempt.

We scrambled to hide the comic books. "You needn't bother, girls. I see those comic books. I'm surprised you would even try to hide them from *me*, Karen."

"Mary Hanford brought them with her; what was I to do when she brought them out?" Karen thrust out her lower lip.

Mrs. Wilner entered the room and stood at the foot of Karen's bed, where a few comic books still lingered. Most had fallen on the floor as we tried to hide them. She seemed very tall.

"It may be true that Mary Hanford brought the comic books, but you, Karen, did not have to read them." Her voice was even calmer than at Thanksgiving. "You, Karen, could have told Mary Hanford that you were forbidden to read them."

"I did, Mommy, I did tell her. She brought those comic books anyway." Karen twisted the edge of her coverlet. I stayed quiet.

"And so, you were obliged to read them, to open their covers, to read them? No, you were not, Karen, and you know that. Mary Hanford may have brought weakness, unwittingly picking up troublesome habits from her family. But, Karen, you read them; you read them, and no one forced you." She repeated "you read them" about fifteen times.

"It's important to take responsibility for one's actions," Mrs. Wilner went on, although Karen was already crying. "One can never tell how one's actions ripple throughout society. This is why some people become leaders and others..." Mrs. Wilner didn't finish her sentence, just let it dribble off. She stared at me, her soft mahogany hair skimming her face as she gathered my comics into a bundle. She was beautiful and calm, too calm. Underneath something bad simmered. I felt like I did when going into Villa Hugel that though everywhere was beautiful, sometime, somewhere, something was going to explode. When Mrs. Wilner left, she took the comics. I knew I would never see them again.

Daddy didn't drink at Wilners because they never drank, but when we got back to Essen, he drank more. And as he drank more, he went on as usual about the pope, Truman, Krupp—only now he spoke more about MacArthur and McCloy. I always remembered them because they both begin with Mc. I knew by then that we were in a war with Korea, and that MacArthur was a soldier running it. How he acted interested everybody—except for me because I still hated the word "Korea." Only later did I learn that the war that had begun a week after my tenth birthday concluded in a stalemate after Truman removed MacArthur from command. Daddy's fears of being sent to Korea were realistic.

Of course, I knew nothing about McCloy and the controversy that surrounded him. I learned later that although he was the civilian commander of the American zone, he had shared a box with Hitler at the Berlin Olympic Games in 1936, and, according to some, advised Benito Mussolini. But the most controversy occurred when McCloy granted amnesty to Alfried Krupp and later restored to him his wealth, on condition that he promise never to make any more weapons, a promise made to be broken. Only a few years after his release, Krupp was again one of the richest men in the world. McCloy's reasons for Krupp's release remain shadowy, as government records on McCloy are still classified as top secret.

Afterwards, as Daddy's rants about Sid Wilner, MacArthur and McCloy increased, I thought about Karen's mother and about what might be under, over, or through Villa Hugel. All disapproval blended into whatever lay about and through Villa Hugel. But it didn't make sense. After all, Villa Hugel was not bombed out, like the other buildings, no matter what was under it.

Eventually, it dawned on me that Daddy was now on the wrong side of something, but I didn't know what. I figured this out because of the serious conversations that Daddy and Sid Wilner had when we were there. Also, they didn't go out to other people's parties as much as in Essen, and we never went back to the Wilner's house for dinner, although that might have been because of me. But maybe it wasn't my fault. Daddy was getting even more upset than usual. His rants included McCloy even more.

"Now McCloy claims all hell will break loose unless…" He would lean back and lace his fingers. Daddy's tone indicated he was considering what McCloy said or did, but that he didn't necessarily agree. "When McCloy was assistant secretary of war, he opposed the plan to bomb railroads leading to Auschwitz.

Imagine the lives that could have been saved..." and then Daddy would veer off onto another topic.

I didn't know what he was talking about, only knew that whatever side he took, he would have thought it right, like I had done in the film room. Maybe I should have protested in a better way. So, maybe Daddy should have done so too.

When Mommy found out about the comic books, she didn't say much; I was surprised. Such misbehavior usually resulted in a lecture or even a spanking. Instead, all was quiet on our way home, too quiet. Mommy and Daddy didn't even speak to each other.

Back in Essen, Daddy's rants increased, especially about McCloy and a little about MacArthur. I wondered if it were because of the comic book crime—but deep down I knew it wasn't. The comic book crime was only a reflection of something bad that had happened in Frankfurt. I knew this because Daddy went on and on about MacArthur or McCloy, but now he included Sid Wilner, whose eyes had gone from sad to really, really cloudy when we left.

The rants got longer and more boring. Mother sat there, listening, knitting, enduring, while I made any excuses to go upstairs to read.

One night, Daddy was ranting about McCloy as a "goddam liar," and the "Holy Father" as....when he stopped mid-sentence and said to Mommy, "Frances, must you keep on with that annoying 'clackclackclack'?"

She looked up. "What clackclack?"

"That blasted knitting you're always doing. Don't I make enough money to buy you and Mary Hanford quality woolen scarves?"

"Of course, you do, but...."

"And don't I provide a comfortable place for you to live, food to eat, clothes for you and Mary Hanford?" He was morphing into a lawyer rant.

"Yes, but...." Mommy wavered. "I need to do something with my hands."

"What is this 'but,' Frances? I didn't get married to have your attention elsewhere. I have important things to work out and talking them out with you is the safest way. What is this need to do something with your hands? You are not a sharecropper's wife who needs to make her family's clothes. If you need to do anything, it is to listen to your husband." If he had ever worked out a solution during these rants, I hadn't seen it.

"Frances, I want you to put those damn knitting needles away when I'm talking with you, for good. A husband deserves his wife's full attention. Sometimes with those clacky things, I wonder if you hear a tenth of what I'm saying. Put them away—now."

"Yes, dear." Mommy put her needles and the knitting dripping from them on the end table, but her face was red and she was breathing hard. Then she folded her hands in her lap.

When I heard her say "Yes, dear," I wanted to jump up and scream "No! Don't do it; don't do it." But I didn't. When I went to bed that night I realized I had changed. I was no longer the "Dawn-Bullied Mary," nor the "Better-than-Irmgard-Mary" Then who was I now? After all, I didn't protest out, although I wanted to. But, I knew for sure, I wasn't better than Irmgard—or anyone.

Then HICOG, the High Commission of Germany, said we had to move to Bonn, move away from Essen, away from Villa Hugel, away from Elasse Strasse, just like that. From what I overheard, we had to move because HICOG, was moving from Frankfurt to Bonn. Also, the coal control group was being dissolved, which Daddy referred to as "an outrage." He thought the coal industries should be "socialized" which meant turned over to the German peoples, but instead it stayed American. Daddy said McCloy had questionable connections with "the Reich" before the war and was wrong getting Krupp out of jail. I don't know if that was "the outrage," but I don't think so because I'd heard that before. Anyhow, I was just sad that we had to move, but got better when I found out we would take Emmy with us.

In Bad Godesburg, a suburb of Bonn, we lived in a first-floor, three-bedroom apartment on 19 Europa Strasse, buildings built just for Americans. Emmy lived in the basement. (Did all Germans who worked for Americans end up in basements?) Mommy insisted that Daddy take the best bedroom, I got second best and she the leavings—a "Dawn-Bullied-Mary" thing to do. But even though she gave him the best bedroom, my parents still hardly spoke to each other.

That bothered me that they didn't speak. I wanted to make it better somehow, and I did so unexpectedly.

Our first Easter in Bad Godesburg was sunny and beautiful. By 8:30 I had opened my Easter basket, made myself sick on chocolate eggs and put on my white organdy Easter dress, although we never went to church. Mommy and Daddy were in their separate rooms, maybe still asleep. I didn't know what to do with myself. I recalled the elderly couples walking hand in hand in the forests in Heisingen and knew elderly couples would be out on a fine Easter Day, so I went out for a walk near the Rhine, just to be near them.

But there weren't many people strolling the Rhine at all; maybe because it was still early, and people were in church. I kept walking, hoping to find someone, but didn't. Finally, I went out on it to gaze at the ruined Castle of Drachenfels across the river and daydream about dragons. All I could really see was the ruined stone tower of Drachenfels, not the rest. If I were closer, I could see the water's reflection of the whole castle where St George rescued the maiden. I looked down at the great river's water. Deep, black and calm, it reflected my head and the top part of my dress. When I bent over more, I could see more of the dress and something else. There was movement under the surface, way under. What? A fish, a school of fish? Also something gleaming down there. Treasure? I forgot Drachenfels. There might be treasure right below me. Maybe if I swirled the water, I could see.

I bent forward to move the water, but couldn't reach it. So I bent further and suddenly there was only air and light and space as I tumbled onto a firmish, flimsy surface that did not cradle me, the Rhine.

I was right. Under the surface was more movement; weeds scratched my legs and got caught in my now heavy skirts, but the big action was an undertow. It was fast, fast carrying me away. I swam towards the pier but the undertow was too strong, strong like the strong bad thing running between Sid and Daddy and Mommy. Above was light, but I couldn't get to it. I prayed to something for help. Then I spotted a thin, thin wire going straight down from the pier to somewhere way deep. I needed to swim to that wire, but no matter how hard I paddled, I didn't move far. Try, trying so hard— my lungs felt like they would split open, I inched towards the wire. Kicking off my patent leather shoes helped. I made one last kick which propelled me forward, and I caught the wire.

The wire cut a little as I pulled myself up into the light. When I reached the surface and looked up, I saw an elderly couple staring down at me. "Eine kleinest Machen!" one of them yelled. The old woman put her apron up to her face, but the old man held out his hand. Then both of them pulled me out. I found my elderly couple—or rather they found me.

I was afraid I'd be scolded when I got home because of my ruined dress and lost Mary Janes but when Mommy opened the door and saw me all scraggly, she burst into tears.

"Oh, Darling, what happened? We've been looking all over. Daddy even called the MPs. Why are you wet? What happened?"

"Come in, you'll catch cold." Daddy took the Oriental rug on the back of our sofa and put it over me. It was heavy and really didn't help. "You must have fallen in the Rhine."

I nodded.

"At least, you're safe. What an irony. I couldn't have stood it. Better a lost job than a lost daughter." Behind his glasses, the rims of his eyes were red.

"You must get out of those wet clothes and take a hot bath right now. And then you're to stay inside today. Do you understand?" Mommy said.

"Come into the living room, when you have her settled, will you, Frances?"

When I got out of the tub and was drying off, I heard them in the living room.

"How do you suppose she got out, Frances?" Daddy said.

"She's not a dog, Frank. She's an eleven-year-old girl. She can unlock any door."

"I don't think she did it on purpose," Daddy said, lacing his fingers. "Didn't she get any rescue training in that British Girl Scout thing?"

"I'm sure she did, Frank, but ..."

On and on they went. Hashing and rehashing possible scenarios of how and why I had fallen into the Rhine, what might have happened and how glad they were I was safe. Then they began talking about other things, like a new job for Daddy. Mission accomplished. Attention for me, Mommy and Daddy speaking to each other again. When I went to bed that evening, they were still talking about buying Daddy a new suit when they got back to the states.

"After all, Frank, you may need a new suit for interviews."

"If I get any interviews."

"Of course, you will get interviews, Dear."

"This job was only temporary; we mustn't forget that."

"Right. We won't forget, but Frank, we need to give some thought to getting Emmy a place. After all...."

I went to my room, hoping they kept it up.

And Mommy and Daddy did keep talking, only not much, not until one night Daddy said, "Frances, the trouble between us is that we have nothing in common. I go to work and you take care of Mary Hanford and do whatever else you do."

I was shocked that he even spoke of "the trouble between us," but Mommy took it in stride. "It certainly wouldn't hurt if we did something together besides just talk in the evenings." Mommy stuck out her jaw and cocked her head. I knew she meant "besides just talk and drink," but Daddy didn't pick up on it.

"What was that camera your sister-in-law, Mildred, got involved with? It took some splendid pictures, and I believe it was German. Do you remember, Frances?"

"Yes, it was a Leica."

"I hear those are very expensive," Daddy said. "We must do some research, find the best value."

I went to bed but knew the conversation would last way late. It had that tone. The next day Mommy said she and Daddy had decided to take up photography and maybe buy a Leica, if it turned out to be the "best camera." The next weeks were full of discussions about which camera was better, Leica or some other kind. Then, after they decided to buy a Leica, it was the same thing all over again about which accessories to buy to go with the Leica. Daddy still drank, but when he began his Mc rants, Mommy changed the subject to Leicas. They were spending wads and wads of money on Leica to stay together, but I knew it wouldn't work. I thought only Daddy's stopping drinking would work, because every day seemed to go well when he wasn't drinking. Yet, once he had that first martini, he seemed to need more and more. Sometimes he didn't go to work for days. But tee-totaling never seemed an option to either one of them. So I just tried to ignore them and busy myself in books or with Emmy until I made some friends.

Now I wonder if he'd gotten sober then whether it would have made much difference in their happiness. It certainly didn't when he sobered up the last few years of their lives. They were as separate then as they were when in Germany. Still, I clung to the fantasy.

Emmy seemed glad enough to show off her progress in cleaning out cabinets, bleaching sheets and ironing. One Sunday, when I was especially bored, I went down to the basement where she ironed and goaded her with sensitive questions like, "Why don't you marry your fiancé who is in Argentina? Can't you get a visa? Do you love him? You must not love him."

Most of the time, she would just fix her hawk eyes on me and tell me to leave the room, but this time it was different.

"He is a very nice man," Emmy said.

"Then why is he in Argentina? Maybe Daddy could get him out for you; get him back here and you could get married."

Emmy made a noise. I couldn't tell whether it was a deep chuckle or a sob. She didn't turn towards me. Something told me to let it go, so I did.

The Leicas kept conversation going for my parents.

"Should we put up the tripod, Frank?"

"Certainly, Frances." And she would struggle to set it up.

"And let's use that extra lens; it's cloudy out."

Then Daddy would, but Daddy seemed to get more and more upset. He started pacing up and down in the evenings and pulling at his crotch. I hated that.

Mommy told me I was becoming a woman now and she wanted me to have fun because she wasn't allowed to because she was a preacher's kid. She bought me my first lipstick, a "clear red" and had my fingernails done at a place made for military wives. But I really wasn't any different, only taller. Boys were still awful, but lipstick was fun and I tried it on many different ways. The whole new scene called "Becoming a Woman," began to replace Emmy as a way to forget Essen and Daddy who was getting angrier and angrier. So I delved into lipsticks, bubble baths, and manicures and "women's magazines" from the PX. It was all very interesting, but silly in some ways. One *Good Housekeeping* beauty column read, "Do all your grooming chores on Saturday, so as to keep a mystique for your husband." That seemed stupid, because a husband would be around on a Saturday especially.

One day I came back from school and both Mommy and Daddy were waiting for me, arms crossed, scowls, and anger shooting out from Daddy like the poison arrows I'd read about in Social Studies. I had done something, something very bad. They wouldn't tell me what. I confessed the comic book sin. It went right over them—Daddy getting more and more enraged. "Do you realize what you've done, Mary Hanford?"

Finally, it came out. I had left my lipstick in a pocket. Emmy had done the laundry and the lipstick had made Daddy's shirts pink or red. Terrible. Both of them looked at me as if I had ordered the holocaust. The other clothes must have been ruined too, but they weren't mentioned. "I'm sorry, I'm sorry," I said, but nothing did any good. It would cost money to fix or maybe buy more clothes, but they acted like I'd killed someone. Finally, I sneaked off, just after Daddy had his third bourbon. And was what I had done really so bad?

A few weeks later, I did another bad thing. It might not have been considered so bad if Daddy wasn't so upset about his job, but then no one made that connection. In our spacious apartment at 19 Europa Str. was a shower, a shower with the bathtub. I'd never had a shower, only baths—didn't remember even seeing one and was delighted by it. Also, in my diversion into womanhood, one thing was clear. Women were supposed to be clean and fragrant, so when I showered I stayed in a long time soaping myself. But one morning my long shower kept Daddy from taking his shower and almost made him late for work. "Wait until I get home," he snarled, running out the door while putting on his hat.

What would he do to me? Memories of when I was five and we lived in Richmond came back. Daddy would threaten to spank me on "General Principles." I would protest, "I haven't done anything bad." He would retort, "You will; you will." Was this the "You will" time? I was a second offender: first the lipstick crime, now the shower. The "General Principles" had become specific crimes. I hid in the bedroom when he came home, but Mommy called me out and told me nothing really bad would happen to me. Daddy had calmed down and was upset really because he was worried about MacArthur and the McCloy betrayal. Those two names again. I decided to find out the big deal.

"What is this Truman/MacArthur trouble?" I asked Daddy later.

"You know there is a war on in Korea, Mary Hanford?" I nodded. "Well, President Truman and General MacArthur had a disagreement about how the war should proceed."

"What was the disagreement?"

"MacArthur wanted the army to penetrate into North Korea, the enemy. Truman thought that was not wise. They could not come to an agreement. So President Truman ordered General MacArthur home."

"Home?"

"Back to the United States."

"You mean he lost his job?"

Daddy nodded. I didn't dare ask if MacArthur losing his job had anything to do with our going home.

"Who do you think was right?" I asked.

"I think Truman was right, Mary Hanford." That figured. Daddy would think so because he was always concerned with the right thing. Killing more people would not be the right thing.

"Okay, thanks. What about the other Mc person?"

"She means McCloy," Mommy wheezed from her easy chair. She had caught a cold.

"Oh, McCloy. I have no opinion, Mary Hanford," he said. But I knew he did.

Daddy's shoulders drooped and he shuffled towards his room. "I'm going to read a little before turning in. People have underestimated Trollope. I'm glad to have discovered him." The way Daddy moved reminded me of captives walking the plank. Something was over, and it wasn't his fault.

I turned twelve in that apartment, but it was nothing special. That birthday garden party in Essen seemed like a far-away fairy tale. The flat feeling birthdays usually brought felt comfortably familiar. Besides we were going back to the USA, and that had to be great. I wondered where home would be this time. It didn't matter really, if my parents were happy, and they seemed to be in Essen, relatively anyway. So what if Daddy and Mr. Wilner didn't get along. The Wilners were strange anyway. After all, Daddy had won over Krupps and made the Germans warm; that was the important thing.

But why did Daddy look so sad? It seemed that Emmy, parties, Joey, Irmgard, Kristal, the pool and Herr Prusnat's roses and fountain were being funneled into a machine which distilled all the good into strong sadness.

I had a serious discussion with Mommy. "I know Daddy worked for the coal control group. But I thought he was also supposed, in part, to dismantle Krupp, find money. Wasn't that the reason he worked in Villa Hugel?"

Mommy nodded.

"Then why is he so sad?"

Mommy went behind me and tied my sash. I had a feeling she wanted to cry and didn't want me to see her. "Because Krupp is bigger than ever now. Bigger than ever."

Something about the way she sighed made me not ask anything more. Politics were crazy, and now I knew that no one nationality was all good or bad but didn't dare announce it. Still, I held a grudge against whomever or whatever was making Daddy sad.

Chapter Fourteen

Boat Ride Home

We were to return home first class on the maiden voyage of the S.S. United States. This, I understood, was a very big deal because the ship could cross the Atlantic in only three days and was reputed to be elegant. We were going First Class. Margaret Truman was also going on the boat, so Mommy said the ship had to be almost perfect for the president's daughter to choose it.

Of course, we had spasms of packing the last few days before we left. Mommy made me throw out a lot of stuff she originally let me pack. I went along with it, until she came to the wooden pencil box with German kids painted on it.

"No, Irmgard gave me this; I want to bring it." It also had the same red toadstools with white spots that I had once thought indicated fairy rings, but I didn't tell her this.

"Sorry, Honey. But no wood's allowed." She explained wood was prohibited on the boat, so it could never catch on fire. The no-wood policy was part of what made the S.S. United States grand. "So hand it over, Mary Hanford. Some little German girl can use it."

"No."

One thing I had learned: German pencil boxes were more sturdy and more interesting with their ubiquitous pictures than any pencil holders I'd come across. The British had no pencil boxes, and the Americans had just transparent plastic envelopes. Also, it would remind me of red cabbage, and my friends.

"For God's sake, give it to me, or I will….." She frowned, dreaming up a punishment.

Frontal resistance was futile. "At least let me give it to Krystal. It won't bother me so much if I give it to a friend. You know she'll use it."

"Oh, all right," Mommy shrugged. "Just make sure you do it. Getting rid of that bunged up box is a small price for riding on such a grand ship.

I'd never been on a ship so wouldn't know the difference between an ordinary ship and a grand one. Somebody said the S.S. United States wasn't as nice at the Queen Elizabeth, but we couldn't get booked on that one.

Our ship was to depart from Le Havre, France, so Herr Prusnat drove us to Le Havre. The car was to be sent back on another boat. To get to Le Havre, we went through Paris, which was supposed to be great, but wasn't. The whole city seemed depressed, not the "gay Paree" Mommy used to joke about, maybe because it was cold and rainy the whole day we were there. Strangely, France seemed to be sadder than Germany. Paris was clean but there were hardly any cars or bicycles. I saw people rushing to a market stand, even in the rain, that had a sign advertising "oeufs" like "oeufs" were diamonds or something. Near a building, a man was playing an accordion under an awning, but no one smiled or even paid attention. In fact, even the music was sad, matching the people. Daddy said Germany was in better shape because of the Marshal Plan.

We didn't have much time for sightseeing, but did go to a park which had statues of women circling it. These, Mommy said, represented France's regions. They were all beautiful except for one which I couldn't see because it had black fabric draped all over it. Mommy said that statue represented Alsace Lorraine which Germany had captured during the war, but then had to give it back to France. The statue was still draped in black because France still mourned that Alsace Lorraine had been grabbed by Germany. But it was almost eight years after the war. Why couldn't people forget it?

Once we reached Le Havre, we boarded the ship immediately and went to find our stateroom. When I saw our luggage already in the stateroom before we even got there, my stomach clenched. I wanted to cry. We were going, really going. I hid how I felt because if Mommy or Daddy knew how much I wanted Emmy or Irmgard, their feelings could be hurt.

So instead I concentrated on the famous ship. The S.S. United States was truly grand, like several elegant hotels put together. But I did see wood, a piano! Naturally, I pointed it out that there was wood, and I should have been allowed my pencil box. Mommy said that before the ship set out, someone had doused it with gasoline and lit it. If it didn't burn, then it proved the piano was truly fire resistant. And it didn't burn, so was allowed.

"Can you say the same about your beloved pencil box? That it wouldn't burn?" she asked.

She had me there.

Actually, the boat seemed made of glass, metal and spun glass, especially the curtains. There were floors and decks with great round windows. Our stateroom was below the main deck and had twin beds with nice bedspreads and a foldout bed high up attached to the wall, like a bunk. The common rooms were huge and decorated in different colors. My favorite was one in bright blue with a kind of wall with a world in bright blue on it, also in turquoise. One bar had little tables with orange chairs, much prettier than Heinz's dark-brown bar in Ayre House. The main deck had squares with numbers drawn on them, like in Hop Scotch. But instead of hopping on the squares, people pushed on them with little block-like things attached to long poles. The game was called Shuffleboard, I guess because of old people who couldn't hop but could shuffle. Other people sat in long chairs called "deck chairs," all wrapped up in blankets. They either read or just watched the sea. Reminded me of a hospital.

So one day, I decided to explore deeper. After all, most of the floors were the same things, staterooms, dining and dancing rooms, and decks. What was beyond them? Mommy always let me roam because even though I got lost a lot, I always found my way back.

First, I went down pairs of elegant stairs, until there were no more. But I looked around and saw a "stairs" sign, so opened that door. There were stairs all right, but narrow ones made of steel bars—not solid. As I went down, the steel stairs began to curve, like that curving stairway in Villa Hugel's great room. It got darker, damp and smelly. There were signs in English saying "do this; don't do that." I kept climbing down and down until a man who looked like a worker because of his overalls and sweat spotted me.

"Hey, Girlie, what are you doing down here?" His voice was so rough, I got scared.

"Nothing," I said.

"That's a whole lot of nothing to be doing in that linen dress. Do you know where you are?"

"I think so but not sure. I think I'm at the bottom of the boat."

He laughed. "Well, you're close. Why would you want to come down here?"

"To see what's down here and how the boat works." I hadn't thought that far but felt I should say something.

"Ah, a mechanic in white skirts. Well, see those dials?" He pointed to a wall across from us. "Those dials are what help propel the boat. My job is to make sure they work right." The dials looked like those the navigator showed me on the plane we came overseas on. "This here ship is made according to Navy rules; it's a lot more complicated than the average ship. Has two separate engine rooms."

"Why does it follow Navy rules? Nobody here is in the Navy."

"Well, Miss Smarty Pants, this ship can be turned into a Navy ship!"

"Huh?"

"Yeah, turned into a fighting vessel if need be. We just don't broadcast it to the world." He grinned. "It's a little like being in disguise."

"But the war's over," I said.

"War's never over, Curly Locks, not really." He turned towards me. "So that's what I'm doing while you people enjoy yourself upstairs, keeping this potential man-of-war cruising." He smiled like someone who had won a contest.

I just stood there.

"You'd better go now, little girl. People will be wondering where you are, especially if you show up with your mouth open, like now. Besides, a squall's coming, and we've got work to do before it hits. Climb back up. I'll make sure I turn away when you start climbing, so you don't have to worry about your skirt."

I hadn't even considered my skirt, but when I was climbing back, all I could think of was to hope he wouldn't see my panties. Once I turned and looked back. He was across the way, fiddling with the dials.

That day I thought about the unseen people running things, while others had fun and didn't know about dials that had to be turned just right or that a storm was coming. That seemed important somehow. What did the people upstairs think about how things were run? Maybe nothing, just like I didn't think about my skirt until the man said something.

The passengers on the S. S. United States certainly did have fun. Part of it was that they dressed up every night. I liked it because I was allowed to wear pretty pink lipstick and to watch grown-ups dance. Also, the dining room was splendid with red chairs and lots of white tablecloths. There was a great big dance floor and a piano, drums and other instruments. One special night called "Captain's Night" was especially splendid. The captain, sporting a white short jacket with bars on it and white gloves, stood at the entrance to the dining room and shook hands with everyone. Even Mommy and Daddy dressed up, she in a black velvet long gown and he in a tuxedo. We also got to sit at the Captain's Table, I think because Daddy was supposed to be important. Mommy was so excited to sit there, that she barely said anything, just sat and nodded when anyone spoke to her. But later she said we had to leave early because the storm had started, and the ship was starting to rock. I knew it was really because Daddy was drunk and about to go on a rant. I wanted to stay and she let me, but after a little while at the Captain's Table, I got scared without my parents there, so made my way downstairs.

Back in the stateroom, Daddy was ranting about McCloy. Only this time he included Krupp, how because of Krupp, Allies had to destroy seventy percent of coal plants, and that's why Daddy had to run the British/American control group. He was glad to do it, but still our government had failed and made a mockery of his career. McCloy shouldn't have let Krupp out, and it was a disgrace. I had heard it so many times that I couldn't stand it.

"Well," I said, "maybe people were wrong to let him out, but Krupp must have done something right, something special to make up for being bad, or they wouldn't have let him out."

"Mary Hanford, this is the first time I have heard you on this subject." Daddy's eyes opened wider, and he looked at me, really looked at me.

"What did Krupp do to get out?"

"Nothing!" Mommy's voice rose. She was lying in bed, still in her black velvet gown, but fooling around with her manicure set. Clippers and tweezers were on the bed in front of her.

"Don't tell her 'nothing,' Frances. Tell her the truth. Never mind; I will." He peered down at me. His breath smelled like whiskey, and his glasses were so spotty that I wondered how he could see. "Krupp promised the allies that he would never again make munitions." The boat jolted, and he steadied himself by holding on to one of the beds.

"Well, that's good—that's wonderful! No more wars, at least in Germany."

"Mary Hanford," Mommy broke in. "If someone told you that if you promised to read the textbooks, you'd not have to go to school, would you promise?"

"Sure."

"And how much would you read of those textbooks after you got out of school?"

I thought about lying but decided against it. "I'd read for a little while and then stop."

"Why would you stop?"

"Because I'd gotten what I wanted."

"Exactly." She sounded as if I had gotten the right answer on a quiz show. She folded her arms across her chest as if the matter were settled.

Daddy grabbed the air as the boat suddenly gave a violent rock, and then fell on the opposite bed, sitting straight up. "For God's sake, Frances, you simplify everything. A child's promise in order to get out of school is hardly an apt comparison with the Krupp fiasco. By simplifying the issue, you belittle me. And this oversimplification makes you fall for everything, status, fashion, ancestry—all superficial. For example, this Captain's Table nonsense. Perhaps you think dressing up sitting at such a table with the boss decked out in whites and stripes makes you a better person." He grinned; his hazel eyes flickered. "Or maybe a thinner person."

"At least I can still stand up to dance," she retorted. The boat lurched, and she fell back against a pillow onto the other bed. The tweezers and clippers fell to the floor with a tinkling sound. She didn't bother to pick them up.

"That was a dirty dig." He weaved a bit. I couldn't tell whether it was from the boat or the whiskey.

Mommy propped herself up on her elbow. "Well, what do you think you've been giving me all night? Nothing but dirty digs."

I was shocked because I'd rarely heard her speak up that way. I wanted to clap but instead ran out the door. "Going to watch dancing," I called out to them, as I left, but they didn't answer.

Upstairs, everyone was dancing and all looked beautiful as they swayed to the music. When the boat rocked, the pairs adjusted themselves. Every once in a while, waiters carrying drinks would stumble when a wave rocked the ship and stuff would spill all over everything, but most people just laughed. The women in their long gowns were out of a movie; some wore satin in rose, and blue—others wore netty stuff usually black and still others had chiffon, pale yellow and green. The captain had left, so far as I could tell. I sat at a small table in the back and watched. It helped me forget things.

"Would you like to dance?" I heard behind me and turned around. There was a boy! He was tall with a few freckles and light brown hair, and he was old, like fourteen.

"Huh?"

"Would you like to dance?"

"Oh, no—I don't know how—also I get sick." I got up and went to the deck, then ran back down to the stateroom, lurching from side to side as the boat churned, grabbing the rails as I made my way downstairs. As I approached our cabin, I felt nauseous. Just outside our door, I vomited. I felt relieved but also terrible about the smell and wanted to hide, but didn't dare go either inside or upstairs, not with vomit on my mouth and my rotten tasting teeth. I huddled against our door. Then a man in overalls appeared.

"Don't worry," he said as he cleaned it up. "Even the crew is sick." But I did worry anyhow, especially that my parents would find out that I had vomited in front of everyone.

I sneaked open the door; my parents were asleep, so I tiptoed in. I went to bed wondering why I had run away because I liked the boy. Also this was the third night and tomorrow we'd be "home," wherever that was, and I had lost my chance. To me, "home" had been wherever my parents were, but now I dreamed of an American version of seven Elasse Str. Only there would be no stupid parties, rants, French people or whiskey. But I couldn't imagine what an American version would be. I was a little scared that we might live in a half-a-house again with other people who drank, because that's what happened before when Daddy didn't have a job. The best would be a white house with a flower garden in back and trees and bushes, like I'd seen in the movie "Lassie," maybe where whiskey was against the law.

As we pulled into New York harbor, people kept going on the deck to see the Statue of Liberty. I had never seen it, but by the time I got a spot between the crowds who were overhanging the deck, all I saw were a few of the spikes around the statue's head. Liberty had spikes. That seemed important somehow.

"Say, little girl, do you want to see Margaret Truman? She'll be first to get off the boat." I looked up and saw the man who told me to get out of the hull; he was cleaned up and wearing fresh work clothes. I knew Margaret Truman was on the boat but never wanted to see her. Her daddy was president, and I believed that somehow he made my daddy rant. I also believed that her daddy made Krystal's cousin have a black baby and an old German woman live in her own basement, and I wasn't entirely wrong. Every decision Truman made rippled throughout, even, or maybe especially, to those officers who winked at soldiers' "peccadilloes" and who wreaked indirect revenge by forcing widows out of their houses. Although Nazis were bad and Americans had freed everyone, there was more to the "after-war" than just that. Taken by itself that belief was more like movie marquee than the movie itself. Goodness and badness were all mixed up. Nothing was really clear. Margaret Truman might be important and a singer, but she and her president daddy were part of the spikes. I shook my head.

"But, Honey, she's the daughter of the President of the United States. We won the war. Now everyone can be free like us. Don't you get it, victory, freedom?"

Freedom stuff. Seemed like another marquee, not a movie. Surely there must be more to freedom than just winning a war. Freedom, maybe, would be no more wars.

"I know who she is."

He bent down and looked at me almost cross-eyed. "Why are you on this VIP ship if you don't get it?" He had a wrinkled, sad face with blood-shot eyes. "Why don't you want to meet her?"

"I'm shy and don't understand politics," I said.

Actually, I feared that if I met Margaret Truman, I'd blurt out that she was a spike.

The skyscrapers loomed tall and ominous as we pulled into the harbor, darkened by other ships and foul-smelling water. Everyone was laughing and clapping when the fog horn blew, but to me the huge buildings and raucous voices were overwhelming. At least with the rubble in Germany you didn't have to crane your neck to see if any chunk was going to fall on you. You just stepped over it.

Everybody who filed off the gangplank seemed to be met by screaming people, many waving American flags. Mildred, the widow of Mommy's dead brother, the one who died of a heart attack, met us. Nicknamed Tiny, because of her six-foot stature, she loomed over us like a skyscraper decked out by

Bloomingdales. A dead fox around her shoulders pointed its face at us. Her purple-jeweled earrings and white gloves that came up to her navy-suited elbows, sparkled against the iron ships and fog grey day. As she hugged each one of us, she squealed, "Oh, Frances; oh, Frank; oh, my God. Thank God....what you must have gone through, and Korea....Oh, my God. You actually escaped. You're back in the land of the free!" Then she turned towards me. "Mary Hanford, you never wrote me!" She pinched my cheek.

"I'm sorry." Guilt crept up my throat. I didn't' remember her.

"Oh, never mind, Brat." Aunt Tiny hugged me, and I smelled roses on her skin. "Now, Frank, tell me what it was really like."

But Daddy was already striding to a street to hail a cab. We got into a yellow cab and went to Aunt Tiny's apartment in Brooklyn, which was as glamorous as its owner. A white satin sofa, tiffany lamps and black-and-white photographs of people in ebony frames adorned the tiny living room. The bathroom had mirrored tissue boxes and lotion holders, plus a pink satin pillow that somehow attached to the back of the tub. I was dazzled by both the person and the place, so resolved to stay quiet.

Aunt Tiny poured from a faceted crystal decanter. "You all must need a drink. And yes, Frank, I am a Leica fan. Not too shabby a gadget, as you can see on the walls. We can swap Leica stories." Some whiskey splashed on an Italian enameled tray. "I've got everything under control." She slapped an oval platter of crackers and cheese on the coffee table. "Even bought some crayons and coloring books for Mary Hanford. We'll just take our time and relax."

You could tell Aunt Tiny never had children, or she would have known I was too old for coloring between the lines of anything. So I just fooled around with the crayons—and drew pictures in the blank margins.

They sat with their drinks, chatting about being tired, the hugeness of New York, and its high prices, the kind of talk that grown-ups use to feel safe with each other. When they finally started talking for real, it wasn't about Daddy's job at all, but about a big-shot who was given a dog named Checkers, and this was very bad. People wanted the man to give the dog back, but he wouldn't, and there had been a fight about it. The man had gone on television to tell people that he was going to keep Checkers, no matter what. That he would have to go on television to justify keeping his dog seemed so stupid that I didn't keep my mouth shut.

"Well, I feel sorry for that poor man. Why would he want to give his doggie back? I didn't want to give Joey to Herr Prusnat, but I had to. That man was just lucky he got to keep Checkers." I drew a puppy in the margins of the coloring book.

"It's not the same thing, Mary Hanford. If you're going to comment on politics, you should know what you're talking about," Daddy said, tipping up his glass to get the last of his drink. "Nixon should never have accepted the dog in the first place. He took it from someone who would then expect a political favor, regardless of the country's best interests. He should have given the dog back immediately and not gone on television to soft soap the public."

"What's 'political favor?'"

"It means doing a favor for someone, usually in secret, that is not given to others. It's not fair and often illegal." Daddy got up to refresh his drink, not waiting for Aunt Tiny to fill it up for him.

I remembered Gordon and Lucinda throwing stones at me and Anne. "But sometimes there's not enough to go around, and you have to choose with whom to share."

"Certainly, that happens, but that's not a political favor. A political favor means doing something that looks legitimate on the surface but has another, usually sinister, motive underneath," Daddy's voice rose. "It means doing something selfish and sneaky while trying to look honest."

I remembered Dawn's squealing on us and claiming to do it out of loyalty to her countrymen, when she just wanted to hurt me. "I think I get it."

"Frank wouldn't even accept a gift, no matter what," Aunt Tiny said. "Pipe said his brother-in-law was 'righteous overmuch.' Ecclesiastes was Pipe's favorite book in the Bible. Pretty interesting for an atheist, huh? Your Methodist preacher father taught Scripture well." Aunt Tiny chortled. She had downed three drinks without eating any crackers.

"Too well." Mommy looked at her lap.

"So, the man getting to keep Checkers was getting away with something?"

"Yes, Mary Hanford," Daddy mumbled. He sounded like someone announcing a death,

"We regret to inform you...."

"Maybe political favors is what let Krupp out of jail with just a promise?"

Aunt Tiny and Mommy looked at each other and then nodded.

"Not so fast, ladies," Daddy said. "You have no right to judge without evidence." He turned to me. "We do not know that, Mary Hanford. It is merely speculation." He leaned back in his chair and folded his hands into a pointy triangle.

Mommy swigged her drink and lit a cigarette, then half-closed her eyes.

"Your father wouldn't have accepted a dog, even if you begged for it; he wouldn't even accept a fruit basket, even if we were hungry. He didn't want anyone or anything to besmirch his name. He is much too upright for that." Her tone was like that when talking to Mme. Pointelle.

Underneath the sweetness ran a river of something dark, something spoiled. I remembered the ship's storm and my throwing up. For a minute, I was scared.

"Upright, yeah, like a Hoover. He sucked up all the political dirt." Aunt Tiny roared at her joke. "And maybe that's the reason he doesn't have a job."

"And maybe it was."

"Frank sucks us all up," Mommy said.

"I'm not sucked up," I blurted out.

"You will be; you will be. All of us, everything I worked for will be forgotten. Just wait."

Daddy's head slumped on his chest.

"Time for a nap, Frank." Mommy stubbed out her Chesterfield and went towards him to help him out of his chair.

"Just wait," he mumbled as they went off to bed. "Just wait."

So I waited and waited. In the meantime, I married, divorced, bore and raised children, professed at a college, even bought that lotion Mommy said was too expensive but which didn't smell as good as sixty years ago. Krupp sneaked in the back door of industry and again became worth billions. There've been other wars and scandals. But when I fetch hairpins from the pencil box I smuggled in or wear my Christmas watch, I know I am not so sucked up that I cannot tell our stories, or Emmy's or Irmgard's or Krystal's or any of us who muddled through those scrambled times. Just as Villa Hugel's portraits still stand, so our echoes ricochet off the pool's green and white tiles. Just listen. You will hear us.

Other books by Mary Hanford
(formerly Mary Bruce)

Dr. Sally's Voodoo Man

In large part, Dr. Sally accepts a Fulbright assignment to teach American Literature at a university in Yaoundé, Cameroon, Africa to get away from her past and find herself. She feels a strange attraction to Dr. Ako Ibo, professor of neocolonial literature and a writer. Slowly, surely, she is drawn into his sphere of influence, falling under his spell. Strongly disbelieving in magic, she nevertheless falls hopelessly in love with Ako. By the time she realizes she is an unwitting tool in the planned assassination of President Biya, she is already seeking escape from Ako. Now she must elude authorities searching for her, and find a way to flee from the country and save her life.

Here's what established writers are saying about this brilliant first novel:

"…bold exploration of a woman adrift in Africa, caught in the turmoil of her own defeated past and in the possibilities offered by her current swirls of chaos. It's a compelling story, told with authority and grace." Fred Leebron, author of *Out West, Six Figures*, and *In the Middle of All This*

"…a maiden novel rife with compact, memorable word pictures." J. Dwight Dobkins, co-author of *Winnie Ruth Judd: The Trunk Murders*

"…refreshing, well-told story written with a combination of force and sensitivity that captures the wondrous complexities of Africa, its people, and the precious vulnerability of the human experience." Freddie Lee

Johnson III, author of *Bittersweet* and *A Man Finds His Way*

"…an incomparable source of information on the African experience. After reading the book, I felt as if I had been on a trip to Cameroon." Alma H. Bond, Ph.D., author of 10 books, including *Who Killed Virginia Woolf?*

"In Dr. Sally, Mary Hanford Bruce has created a complex character as driven by her need for love as she is by her desire to grow. The African jungle is a rich landscape for the desperate search for self-awareness." Dr. Kathleen DeGrave, author of *Company Woman*

This is what J. Clayson BaHons of Cambridge, England, said after reading the author's manuscript: (Clayson is a former bookstore owner in the UK.) "Daring and exhilarating, Dr. Bruce's exciting first novel provides rare and profound insights into the workings of the African mind."

Nearly everyone who has read Dr. Sally's Voodoo Man has remarked about Dr. Bruce's ability to create compact, memorable word pictures. Here are some examples:

- She couldn't tell if it were the wine or a memory, but she felt heavy, like air before a storm.
- At home the evening spread before her like a vacant hall, where if she called her name, echoes from the past would answer.
- Greens of all descriptions hung like feather dusters from bamboo poles among clattering, chattering women.
- Her head throbbed at the back of her skull, further back than she dreamed a mind went.
- What's the use of a candle if it has no darkness to shed?
- She had a hole in her understanding.

- She felt a tap and swirled around to see a wrinkled woman, who looked like tobacco in a hand-rolled cigarette paper.
- She tried to get up, but her spine forgot to support her.
- Clothes dropped from her like petals.

***

Holding to the Light

Award-winning poet Mary Hanford Bruce explores her awakening consciousness and shares her pain and insights she experienced both in the United States and in the Third World. The original print edition was published after her two years as a Fulbright Scholar in Cameroon, Africa. She is known for her ability to say much in a few words, whether it is showing sorrow, loneliness, pain or wonderment.

A poem from this book:

Flight
If I look for you in the marshes
of a bird reserve,
will I find you
in the wooden blind looking at a grey wren,
or the North Sea staring at gulls?

You are not in the hide, on the sea,
not in my arms. In the room
we shared I look for the hollow of your shoulder,
find only air and the scent

of a blue jacket flapping through airplane doors
sounds of electronic closings sicken me.
That eel we watched gulped by a cormorant,
stalked by a hopeful heron, was a violence
no more true than the way Africa has swallowed you.

Ordering info about Mary Hanford's books, and other good books bearing the UCS PRESS imprint, may be found at www.MarJimBooks.com. UCS PRESS is an imprint of MarJim Books.

UCS PRESS
Small press. Big Reading Value.

www.ingramcontent.com/pod-product-compliance
Lightning Source LLC
LaVergne TN
LVHW051511080426
835509LV00017B/2016